The Sober Journey

A GUIDE TO PRAYER AND MEDITATION IN RECOVERY

DIRK FOSTER

gatekeeper press

Columbus, Ohio

The Sober Journey: A Guide to Prayer and Meditation in Recovery

Published by Gatekeeper Press
2167 Stringtown Rd, Suite 109
Columbus, OH 43123-2989
www.GatekeeperPress.com

The editorial work for this book is entirely the product of the author. Gatekeeper Press did not participate in and is not responsible for any aspect of these elements.

ISBN (paperback): 9781642377699
eISBN: 9781642377705

This book is dedicated to my mother, Jane Foster,
the most compassionate person I know.

And to my wife, Dany Foster, my best
friend, my true love, my beating heart.

CONTENTS

ONE
In the Beginning

TWO
Prayer

THREE
Prayer with Focus

FOUR
Meditation

FIVE
Meditation with Focus

SIX
The Big G Word

SEVEN
Prayers

ONE

In the Beginning

"We do not want to be beginners. But
let us be convinced of the fact
that we will never be anything else but beginners, all our life!"
~ *Thomas Merton*

"No matter how much light I carry within me,
there will always be times of feeling lost, being
confused, and seeking direction.
It is the way of the human heart."
~ *Joyce Rupp*

"We are not human beings having a spiritual experience;
we are spiritual beings having a human experience."
~ *Pierre Teilhard de Chardin*

1

Motel Hell

'm lying face down on the floor of a cheap motel in Los Angeles, my head turned to the side. The room is dark and spinning. I can smell the filthy rug pressing against my cheek. I hear cars passing on the street outside, tires sloshing over the rain-soaked pavement. I attempt to crawl to the bed but my body simply won't function.

My brain is saying, *Crawl!* but my body is saying, *Screw you! I ain't moving!*

I just want to get off the damn floor. I'm trying as hard as I can to reach the bed but it's no use. I start sobbing, whimpering like a wounded animal. I think to myself, *If I lose consciousness I might never awaken.* But I'm so tired. I want to sleep so badly.

I realize I might be dying but there's nothing I can do to stop it. *God, what have I done?*

Then sudden clarity fills my mind. It's like a surge of electricity through my body and mind. I'm totally aware of everything in the room. I'm floating above my body, looking down at myself lying spread eagle on the floor. I know exactly where I am and how I got here.

I remember the entire day and the terrible fight I had with my girlfriend. I remember checking into the motel with the intention of drinking myself into oblivion. I remember every single drink I consumed. I'm completely aware that I am in the throes of alcohol poisoning. I know with total certainty that this is it— this is the night I'm going to die.

The police will find me. The ambulance will haul away my corpse. Someone will have to identify me in the morgue.

As I float above the room, looking down at my own body, I think of my parents. I realize that if I die tonight, they will know that this is how I ended my existence. They, and all the people I love, will fall to their knees in grief and shame. They will suffer the rest of their lives for what I have done to myself and to them. I'm flooded with sorrow and regret.

Then I begin to pray...*God, please don't let me die this way. Please, God. Please, not like this. Let me make it through the night. I want to live. I want to live, God. I don't want to destroy my family. I don't want to hurt my mother and father. God, I need your help. I need your help, God. Help me get through this night so I can start over. Let me begin again. Give me another chance. Please, God. Let me live. Let me begin again. Let me live...*

I pray and pray without stopping. I don't know how long I continue to pray but at some point, I pass out.

I awake in the morning, still on the floor, head pounding, eyes caked shut, stomach burning, feeling like absolute hell.

But I'm alive. Gratitude overwhelms me. *Thank you, God! Thank you! Thank you!*

***

I wish I could claim that I never drank alcohol again after that night. Most people would expect that this type of experience would shock anyone into getting sober. But I can tell you from a great deal of experience that recovery from addiction—especially an addiction that has been cultivated over decades—typically doesn't happen overnight. It often takes many attempts and relapses before the desperation becomes so painful that sobriety becomes a last and final resort.

It's referred to as "the gift of desperation" because desperation is the only thing that brings us to our knees so that we can finally ask for help. Desperation becomes our saving grace.

I struggled to get sober for another year. I went to AA meetings, often drunk. I went to drug counseling with drugs in my system. I went to an acupuncturist to try to stop the urge to drink. I went to a behavioral psychologist. I tried using exercise to avoid alcohol. I tried only drinking on weekends instead of every night, a resolution which lasted only three days. I went on Antabuse, a drug prescribed to stop you from drinking by making you violently sick when you consume alcohol. I drank anyway.

Nothing worked. Nothing stopped me from drinking. Then the gift of desperation descended upon me.

I was driving though Los Angeles one sweltering summer day with a skull-crushing hangover. I knew I had completely lost control of my life. As I came to a stoplight, waiting for the signal to turn, I felt miserable and depressed.

I began thinking about that night a year prior, back at the cheap motel. I remembered my prayers, my pleas to God. I remembered the absolute heartbreak I felt, the guilt and disgust. And I remembered the promise I made to get sober if only I were allowed to live.

The light turned green. Without even thinking about it, I turned left onto Fairfax Avenue instead of going straight in the direction of my dirty shoebox of an apartment. It was like someone else was driving the car and I was just a passenger.

I began driving towards Santa Monica Boulevard, remembering a beautiful Catholic church where I had attended a friend's wedding years earlier. For some reason, that's where I was headed.

Now to clarify, I'm not Catholic, nor was I a religious person. But I had always harbored a secret faith in a Higher Power of some kind, even if I had no idea what that Higher Power was or how to communicate with it. I just always had an innate feeling that I wasn't completely alone in the universe.

As I walked into the church, I felt complete and total discomfort. I felt stupid, in fact. I had no idea what I was doing there or what I was supposed to do now that I had arrived. Thankfully, it was in the middle of the day and there wasn't anyone else there. I had the entire church to myself.

I made my way to one of the pews, sat down and looked up. It was beautiful, quiet and peaceful. I could feel myself begin to relax. I closed my eyes and listened to the silence surrounding me. I didn't realize it then, but this was my first experience with a simple form of meditation. Then I did the unimaginable. I reached down and lowered the prayer bench near my feet.

Instinctively I opened my eyes and looked around to see if anyone else had come into the church. I was embarrassed and didn't want anyone to see what I was doing, as if people in a church would be shocked to see someone praying.

The coast was clear. I slowly lowered myself onto the prayer bench, clasped my hands in front of me, shut my eyes tight, and began to pray.

I had no idea what I was supposed to say or how to pray. So, I just improvised. Silently I rambled on and on for probably fifteen minutes. I asked for help, for peace in my life, for understanding, and for forgiveness. I asked why I was such a raging mess of a human being. I asked *where has my life gone wrong? How can I get it back?*

I prayed and prayed. Mostly, I just asked for help. Finally, I stood up and left the church. I was shaking. My eyes were filled with tears. I stepped out into the warm, bright daylight and immediately sensed that something was different. Something had changed.

There was a shift in the axis of my being. For the first time that I could remember, I felt an enormous sense of relief. I knew, absolutely knew with complete certainty, that I was going to be okay. I could recover. I could heal. I could live the life I was supposed to live. I don't know why I felt that way, but it was as clear as the day.

I called my friend, Guy, who had been working on his sobriety for a while himself, and asked him to take me to an AA meeting. We went to a meeting that night. This time, I wasn't drunk. I listened, I cried and I began the process of recovery. That was over eleven years ago—over eleven years that I've been clean and sober.

Looking back, I now realize that I was brought to my knees--I had reached the point of desperation--not by any one specific event or tragedy, but by a series of events that happened over many years. Like so many people, I had allowed myself to wallow in a lifetime of self-indulgence and self-pity. I had become so spiritually bankrupt that I had lost all control of my life, emotions and my sense of self-worth. I was like an empty shell of a person who needed to be filled with hope, joy and peace. To borrow an overused phrase; I needed to be reborn.

And so my journey began, first by joining a 12-step program, and then by exploring the inner workings of my mind and spirit. What I learned along the way, this journey of discovery that has impacted every aspect of my life, is what I want to share in these pages. Perhaps you too will discover at least some of the serenity and hope that comes from this simple pathway of prayer and meditation that we will explore together.

2

Lost At Sea

have spent the last twelve years exploring prayer and meditation as tools to my recovery and my peace of mind. And the benefits have been unfathomable.

For many years before I got sober, I was lost at sea. I was struggling against powerful currents of fear, insecurity, loneliness, doubt and anxiety. I self-medicated with alcohol and narcotics in an attempt to fill an emptiness I felt in my mind, spirit and soul.

I believe that everyone on the planet feels lost at sea sometimes. Not everyone struggles with substance abuse, and I pray you never do. But self-doubt and spiritual pain are simply a part of being human. No matter how blessed our lives might be, no matter how much success we have, how many friends we have, or how big our house is, we all suffer at times through periods of spiritual and mental anguish. No one is immune to fear, sadness and suffering.

Suffering, it seems, is just a part of being human. Suffering, struggle, failure and pain are intrinsic aspects of life. Often it is pain and struggle that teach us the most valuable lessons we need to learn in order to be happy (as my dad used to say, "Pain builds character"). But for people like me, and perhaps you feel this way too, the instinct is often to swim AGAINST THE TIDE instead of flowing with it like a leaf on a mighty river. Instead of fighting against the powerful current of life, we need to find a way to flow with it in order to enjoy the ride.

If suffering is in fact a part of being human, then there must be a way for us to deal with it and use it to our advantage.

All the major religions of the world have long recognized that suffering is a part of human nature. Consider the following:

- Buddhists believe that to live means to suffer (Dukkha).
- Christians believe we suffer because of our sinful nature (Original Sin).
- Hindus and Buddhists believe that suffering is an inescapable part of life due to improper conduct in our past lives (Karma).

Over the centuries, every religion has attempted to discover effective methods to ease suffering and improve spiritual awareness. What I have learned is that mankind has developed some amazing (and most importantly *non-medicinal*) ways of coping with pain and suffering, methods that are available to anyone searching for relief. And most of these methods, prayer and meditation in particular, are easy to enjoy and can be used, and even mastered, by just about everybody willing to try.

I stumbled upon prayer and meditation through trial and error. I was suffering and needed relief. The recovery program I joined set me on the path of sobriety. The 12-step program was the beginning of my sober journey. I worked very hard on the steps and still use them to this day as touchstones in my sobriety. But prayer and meditation are what sustain me to this day by helping me stay clear-minded, focused, grateful and comfortable in the world. Prayer and meditation are things I do every day, and every day I look forward to my practice even if it's just for a few minutes in the morning, because within those few minutes is where I find so much calmness, strength and *acceptance*.

I've come a long way since I was lying on that motel floor in Los Angeles. Today my life is drastically different. I live near Lake Tahoe with my beautiful wife, Dany, and our amazing dog, Moonpie (yes, Moonpie!). I spend most of my free time fishing and hiking instead of boozing and drugging. I'm healthy and at peace with the world (most of the time). I couldn't be more thankful. And every day, I pray and meditate, and that has made all the difference.

Without prayer and meditation, I would still feel lost at sea, sober or not. For me, prayer and meditation are like harbors in the storms of life—storms that confront each of us. No one is immune to suffering, but prayer and meditation are proven and powerful methods that ease the pain. They can help us find safety and serenity, no matter what the world throws our way. The following are great illustrations of this truth:

- When my father was dying of cancer, prayer and meditation kept me sane and present for my family.
- When I've watched friends die from addiction, prayer and meditation have given me strength to move forward.
- When I've struggled financially, prayer and meditation have helped keep me from panicking.
- When I started my own business, prayer and meditation helped me find the courage to persevere against self-doubt.
- When I decided to leave Los Angeles for Lake Tahoe, prayer and meditation gave me the courage to embark on a new adventure.
- When I thought about asking my wife to marry me, prayer and meditation gave me the courage to trust myself and follow my heart.

These are just a few examples of how prayer and meditation help in my daily life. There are countless other examples.

But how did it happen? How did I discover how to pray and meditate in a way that works effectively and reliably? Figuring it out was the difficult part of the journey.

As I mentioned earlier, the first time I prayed in the church in Los Angeles, I felt like a complete fool. I was embarrassed, even though no one else was around. The first time I tried to meditate, the noise in my brain was so loud I thought I might actually be insane. I call this noise "the Chattering Monkeys," which I'll explain in a later chapter.

Learning how to pray and meditate in a manner that suited me was not easy. In fact, it was often very difficult and extremely frustrating. At other times it was awkward and embarrassing.

The problem was I simply didn't know who to ask about it, or what or how to ask. So, I experimented, read countless books, took classes, and practiced.

One important thing I've learned over years of study and practice is that what works for me might not work perfectly for you.

Prayer and meditation are a lot like religion… All spiritual roads lead to God but not all of us are driving in the same car to get there. You have to find what works best for you.

What I want to do is to offer a simple map to help you start your own journey. Regardless of what anyone tells you, *there is no right or wrong way to pray or meditate*. There is only the way that fits you, brings you comfort, eases your suffering and offers you a sense of infinite hope.

Keep an open heart and mind. Step into your new adventure with a smile and the realization that every day is a fresh opportunity to start over and rejuvenate your life. If you can learn how to flow with the river of life instead of swimming against it, the beauty of being alive will be made more abundantly clear.

3

Spirits in the Material World

et's begin with the premise that we possess a spirit or soul. Yes, we are physical beings with bodies that grow, change and eventually deteriorate and die. We feel pain when we stub our toe. We feel nauseous and tired when we're sick. Our hair turns grey as we age. We enjoy the taste of food and the pleasures of sex. All these things are undeniably true. But there's much more to our experience on earth than our physical bodies.

In order to get the most out of prayer and meditation, it's important to accept (or at the very least *consider*) the idea that there is more to you than just a body made of skin and bones. Your personality, your essence, that indefinable thing called *you* is much more than just a bunch of molecules and atoms slamming together in a cold, random universe. You are life itself, ever expanding, striving, thriving, forever moving forward and upward through infinite changes and possibilities.

You are a *spiritual being,* having a physical experience. This may sound strange at first, like you're an alien (spirit) visiting a planet (your body). But in a way this is true. Our bodies are like vehicles that transport our personalities from one location to another while we're on earth. Our bodies are a part of our life experience, and should be respected and enjoyed for the pleasures they bring. But the essence of who we are as individuals comes from something else; not from our fingers and toes, but from our ideas, thoughts and feelings.

There is a spirit within you that is beyond the physical realm. There is a soul within you that craves something more than just food, sex and other physical pleasures. There is a desire deep within the human soul for understanding and enlightenment, wisdom and love. These things, love in particular, come from a place that cannot be seen, heard or touched. They can only be felt from the inner core of your being. They can only be discovered and experienced through a spiritual journey—a journey that begins with prayer and meditation.

To be clear, I am never going to try to convince you or anyone else to follow a particular religion or set of beliefs. You might already be a Christian, Jew, Muslim or Buddhist. Or perhaps you follow the teachings of Ernest Holmes and the New Thought movement. Maybe you're an agnostic who doesn't know *what* to believe because it's all just too overwhelming and there's no guaranteed certainty.

I believe that religion is an individual choice that should be respected by everyone. How you choose to understand and draw closer to God is entirely up to you. All the major religions grapple with the same basic questions and all have developed some degree of clarity and truth about life and God.

Wherever you fall on the religion spectrum, keep your mind open and available to new ideas and possibilities. You can't learn anything new if you shut down your mind. You can't see the sunrise with blindfolded eyes. The most important thing when starting on a new journey—especially a spiritual journey!—is to keep an open mind and heart. Test new ideas. Consider new information. Find what works and disregard what doesn't work.

It's important to remember that no one has a monopoly on the truth when it comes to religion and spirituality. Yes, there are religious leaders and cultist who will claim they have a direct line to God and only they know the truth. But usually people who make such claims have something to sell or are seeking power and fame.

One of the great elements of Buddhism is an emphasis on belief in the teaching, not the teacher. No matter how charismatic, entertaining, attractive or wise a teacher might be, it's crucial not to become trapped in a cult of personality where the person teaching becomes more important than the teaching itself.

History is filled with the tragic consequences of people following a mesmerizing personality to the gates of hell. Learn from others wherever you can. But recognize when a teacher is offering wisdom and love instead of demanding conformity and blind loyalty.

The most important teacher you will ever find is *you*. Learn to trust your own inner voice. Follow your own spiritual quest instead of adhering to what someone else is telling you. Yes, there are many things you can learn from other people, and I hope I can offer a few kernels of wisdom that will help you move forward in your journey. But you have an inner voice that will teach and guide you more than you can imagine.

There is a spirit within you connected to the infinite. The sage you seek is closer than your own breath. As you move forward and learn more, always listen to the inner voice within you. From your inner voice, you will discover your true spirit as your travel through the physical world.

4

Prayer AND Meditation

You might be curious about why I keep referring to "prayer AND meditation" instead of "prayer OR meditation."

The answer is simple: They complement each other beautifully, so I like to do them together. In spiritual terms, prayer and meditation are the perfect marriage.

You can do them separately or together. It's entirely up to you. But my preferred routine is to combine prayer and meditation into one single experience. This is especially helpful if you're extremely busy or have limited time. It's also ideal if you can't commit more than a few minutes per day to your practice.

I usually start my morning with a combination of prayer and meditation before I do anything else. I sit on my couch in a comfortable position and focus on my breath or a simple mantra for ten to fifteen minutes. Then I begin my prayer, which usually lasts for a few minutes. The length of time you spend is not very important right now. You can do it for longer or shorter periods, depending on your circumstances or mood that day.

Later on, I will discuss in more detail how I practice my own prayer and meditation every morning, as well as throughout the day and evening. I'll also discuss the amount of time to spend in prayer and meditation. But for now, just realize that you can do both at the same time, or do them separately, depending on your personal preference. But doing them together is efficient, saves time and deepens the experience and benefits of both.

In many ways prayer and meditation are very similar. Consider how each can be a benefit by:

- Offering an opportunity to center our minds and focus our thoughts, emotions and desires
- Helping us to connect with the spiritual side of life
- Activating our innate need for communion with the infinite
- Helping to clear our minds and open our hearts
- Providing moments of peace and tranquility
- Allowing us a chance to explore our own minds
- Reducing fear and even physical pain
- Infusing us with energy and joy
- Creating a an atmosphere of acceptance

Both prayer AND meditation are simple ways to settle your mind, expand your understanding of who you are and how your mind works. In addition, it's an opportunity to explore transcendence.

Transcendence is defined as "extending or lying beyond the limits of ordinary experience." Another way to express transcendence is to say "beyond the here and now" or "touching the infinite." However you want to phrase it, transcendence is our opportunity to explore the mysterious and mystical side of life which begins on the inside, within our own mind and spirit.

What's most important is finding a way to incorporate prayer and meditation into your daily life. Whether you create a morning routine or constantly change your routine based on your mood that day, it doesn't really matter for now. Just start your practice. Eventually you'll find what suits you best.

5

Keep it Interesting

Have you ever repeated a single word or phrase over and over until you suddenly forget what it means? When I was kid, I had an obsessive-compulsive habit of repeating a single word in my head. I would lock onto one word and say it nonstop until I forgot what it meant. It amused the hell out of me.

Granted, I was sort of an odd duck as a child, but I know many people who have experienced this strange occurrence. It's called "semantic saturation," a psychological phenomenon in which repetition causes a word or phrase to become temporarily meaningless.

Repetition of anything can become dull and meaningless, much like words in your head. Eating the same food every day can become boring very quickly. Listening to the same music without variety can become very tedious. Doing the exact same exercise at the gym every day is not only boring but also becomes less and less effective over time. In fact, if you want to build a stronger, healthier body you absolutely must change up your routine, otherwise your muscle and cardio improvement will plateau.

Prayer and meditation are no different. It's important to occasionally change things up. You don't have to do something drastically different every day, but there are times when variety in your practice is essential to keeping it fresh, interesting and effective.

Over the years, I have tried many different styles of meditation. These include sitting meditation, walking meditation, reclining meditation and yoga meditation. I've even practiced fishing meditation, my personal favorite, which I will discuss in a later chapter. But the point I want to make is this: you don't have to do just one type of meditation or prayer, or combination of the two, all your life. I encourage you to try a variety of methods over time. Some you will enjoy, while some you won't. But keep exploring, because that's half the fun.

All the major religions have developed some form of meditation. Of course, the most famous is Buddhist meditation, which offers a wide variety of styles and methods. But there are many other forms of meditation including Hindu meditation, Christian meditation, and Sufi meditation. In almost every community in Western culture you can also find various *guided* meditations without any religious connection.

The same thing holds true with prayer. In the stereotypical image of prayer, we often see a child on her knees, hands pressed together, staring up to heaven. This is a wonderful way to pray, and one I often use, but it's by no means the only way to pray. I often pray while lying in bed. Walking prayer is extremely effective and often allows for a much deeper level of contemplation. Prayer during exercise is one of my favorite methods. Yoga in particular can be one of the best times to pray.

You can pray and meditate indoors or outdoors, in a crowded room or an empty room. You can do both in a mansion or homeless shelter, in a tree, on a rock or on a yacht, on a beach or in a forest. Anywhere and everywhere can provide an opportunity to pray and meditate. I've often slipped away from a party or crowded event (not my favorite places to be) and found an empty room (often a bathroom) to spend a few minutes in prayer and meditation. Since I sometimes struggle with social anxiety, this is often the only way I can get through certain situations.

I once read about a woman who would place a cushion on the sidewalk in the middle of Time Square in New York and meditate for up to an hour. Think about that! Thousands of people pass through Time Square every day, tourists, business people, street performers. Cars are honking. People are talking and sometimes yelling at each other (we are talking about New York). All the while a woman is able to sit in the middle of all the chaos and successfully meditate and find tranquility amidst the mayhem. Now if that's not a way to keep it interesting, I don't know what is!

I'm not suggesting you need to go sit in the middle of a crowded street every time you pray or meditate. But it's good to change things up occasionally.

Variety, as they say, is the spice of life. Variety in prayer and meditation will keep you more interested and will enhance your experience.

6

Frustration

'Ve always enjoyed card games. As a small boy, I played card games with my dad and brothers and loved poker in particular. One of my favorite card games is Texas Hold'em Poker. It's a highly complex game that requires enormous amounts of study, concentration and strategy. It's a lot like playing chess, but instead of playing against one opponent, you're playing against eight or nine. It's a very difficult game and takes a lifetime to master. It's also a very social game, offering a great opportunity to meet many intelligent and interesting people.

Recently I was playing Texas Hold'em and growing increasingly frustrated by the hands I was being dealt. No matter what I did, I couldn't win a pot. Sitting next to me was Bo, a man I've played with many times over the last few years. Bo could tell how frustrated I was getting.

He leaned over to me and, in his thick Russian accent, said with a smile: "Patience is the best teacher. Time is the best judge."

It was exactly what I needed to hear at that moment. Poker, like so many things in life, requires a great deal of patience and time if you want to improve. Prayer and meditation also require patience and time before you will be comfortable in your practice.

Frustration is one of the most difficult challenges we encounter when we're learning to pray and meditate. Meditation in particular can be challenging at first, but you have to keep trying and not take yourself too seriously as you learn. Don't let frustration block your path.

When I first began to meditate, one of the biggest challenges I encountered was all the noise in my head. It was overwhelming. I tried to keep my eyes closed and focus on my breath. The problem was that there was so much chatter, and so many passing images, that I couldn't focus or calm down. In fact, I found it a little frightening.

Being new to meditation, I was startled by how much was swirling around in my brain. And I was taken aback by a lot of the thoughts, ideas and images in my head. They were often pretty negative. This would change over time but at first, I thought that I might be crazy. It was disturbing and incredibly frustrating.

I was coming off a 30 year bender of booze and drugs and had accumulated and stored an enormous amount of negativity, sadness, anger and resentment. The thoughts and images in my head were a reflection of my emotional state of being. When I would attempt to sit and focus on my breath, my mind would swirl with strange and hostile ideas, ideas that I didn't want to face or understand. They were just too overwhelming. It was truly shocking to realize how insane my thinking had become over the years. Closing my eyes was to confront a nightmare. When it came to sleeping, I would usually just watch television until I dozed off which saved me from having to bear witness to what was going on in my mind.

I'll never forget the way my friend Paul, an early mentor of mine, described his own experience with meditation. He said that it was like visiting a multiplex cinema that was showing a dozen different movies at the same time, and running from one theater to the next in a frantic attempt to watch and understand each movie. Since that's impossible to do, over time you have to learn to focus your attention on just one movie at a time and let the others go.

This metaphor so perfectly described my own brain activity, it made me laugh. And the laughter is what helped me learn to not take it all so seriously and just keep moving forward with my practice.

Yes, the images and thoughts in my brain could be disturbing and frightening. But they were just thoughts, nothing more. If I could learn to accept them like harmless mental movies, I could then begin to settle down and successfully focus on my breath and let the negativity slip peacefully away.

Learning to pray and meditate can and will be frustrating at first. I promise you that. If you're new to this, you will discover that your mind is filled with a cacophony of noise, sights and ideas, just like multiple movies all playing simultaneously in your head.

But lighten up. Allow it to happen. Smile during the experience.

Have you ever traveled to a foreign country where you didn't speak the language? You arrive and you feel overwhelmed and lost. Frustration can quickly take over your trip. But if you take the right steps, find a good map, find a few people who might understand you, and ask for help, you'll start to enjoy the experience—the sights, the sounds and all the new people surrounding you.

In many ways, prayer and meditation are similar. Don't lose patience. Ease into it, try to relax, and enjoy the experience. And never forget to smile. In time, you'll figure out where you are and start to love the journey.

7

Pathways

For some people the path to spiritual awakening begins in childhood when they attend church or temple with their parents. For others, the journey begins when their world is shattered by tragedy or loss. And for people like me, the journey commences when we realize that the spiritual solution we seek isn't to be found in a bottle.

As I stated earlier, I believe that all spiritual roads lead to God, but not all of us are driving in the same car to get there. There are numerous pathways to awaken your mind and enable you to draw nearer to God, a Higher Power, or the conscious Spirit that permeates the universe.

Prayer and meditation are just two pathways that can help you reach an elevated level of consciousness and find peace of mind. In my experience, these two pathways are the easiest and most reliable. Why? Because prayer and meditation:

- Require no money

- Can be practiced almost anywhere, anytime
- Require no classes or school degrees
- Can be practiced by anyone, regardless of social background or economic condition
- Have no religious requirements
- Require no special props, tools or equipment
- Can be practiced indoors or outdoors, day or night
- Rely only on our mind, body and soul to be successful
- Have been practiced successfully for thousands of years in every known culture
- Are natural gifts that emanate from deep within the human soul

Both prayer and meditation can be practiced through formal ritual or in a more casual setting at home, in your office or outside in nature. It's entirely up to you. I've gone through phases where I prefer a more structured, formal practice with teachers and other students. I've also attended churches and temples in order to learn and worship with others. And I've done a lot on my own. Among other things, I've read books and enjoyed the quiet solitude of home or the beauty of a mountain river while praying and meditating.

The pathways you choose for your spiritual journey are a matter of personal taste. But if you're just getting started, or are unsure of how to proceed, this book is designed to help you begin. It will give you an overview of what prayer and meditation are, how they can benefit your life, what to focus on during your practice and, most importantly, how to have fun and enjoy the ride in whatever "car" you choose.

This isn't a complicated, esoteric subject (although it can be if you wish to pursue a much deeper practice later on). For now, just get started with a few simple steps that are suggested in the following pages. Experiment and try different things. Find what works best for you.

Most importantly, GO EASY ON YOURSELF. Remember, there really is no right or wrong way to pray or meditate. There is just *your* way, the way that fits you, your personality and comfort level.

So how do you get started? What's the first step?

To quote Desmond Tutu, "There is only one way to eat an elephant: a bite at a time." Let's take the first bite.

TWO

Prayer

"*Thank you* is the best prayer that anyone
can say. I say that one a lot.
Thank you expresses extreme gratitude,
humility, understanding."
~ *Alice Walker*

"Prayer does not change God, but it changes him who prays."
~ *Soren Kierkegaard*

"Only in prayer do we achieve that complete
and harmonious assembly
of body, mind, and spirit which gives the frail
human reed its unshakable strength."
~ *Alexis Carrel*

8

What is Prayer?

What is prayer? It seems like such a simple question. After all, prayer is a word everyone has heard, like electricity or air or love. But what *is* prayer and how can it help me improve my life?

That's a question I always asked, long before I began to incorporate prayer into my daily life. As a child, I had an innate belief in some kind of force or personality that surrounded me and kept me safe. I can't explain why I felt this way.

Like I stated earlier, I was not raised in a religious home. So, it was up to *me* to try to answer the questions; *what is this presence I feel? And is there a way to communicate with it?*

One of the best things about early childhood is a lack of self-consciousness. When I was very young, I had no problem talking to God, usually out loud. To me, God felt like a friend who was always there, somewhere, even though I couldn't see him/her/it (I want to clarify that I don't think of God as male or female. To me, God is gender-neutral. I'm not trying to be politically correct by covering all my bases; I just feel that gender is something necessary to human evolution on earth, but probably irrelevant beyond our planet. So, I will sometimes interchange he/she/it when I refer to God.)

We all know about children having imaginary friends that they speak to and play with when they are alone. Maybe you had one yourself. To most children, these friends that can't be seen by anyone else are as real to them as their own parents. They play together, carry on conversations, create games, and provide companionship and comfort.

At some point, however, the child starts going to school and interacting with other children and experiencing the world outside their home. It's usually around this time that the child begins to show less and less interest in their imaginary friend, usually replacing that friendship in the pursuit of human friendship and material desires. The child becomes so immersed in the rituals of socializing that their focus on their "imaginary" friend is replaced by daily interaction with other people.

But what if that communication with an imaginary friend is actually a form of communication with God? What if the conversation the child is engaged in every day is really a form of prayer, wherein the child relies on an innate trust that there is a force or personality surrounding them, and that speaking with that presence is just a natural way of connecting with it?

The presence, or Higher Power, is already there. So, why not talk with it and play with it and allow it to provide comfort and companionship every day? To the child, there's nothing shocking or strange about it; she's just chatting with a friend.

An important part of prayer is a willingness to trust that there is something beyond what we can see and a reliance on what can only be felt through intuition. Can we become childlike again, trusting in an innate sense that there is more to life than meets the eye?

In many ways we are trained to become cynical or doubt the existence of anything that we can't see or touch. We live in a society that is constantly selling us "stuff" and images of things we should own or possess. If we can't see, touch, smell or taste it than what's the point? Billions of dollars are spent every year on advertising all the latest gadgets we need to own in order to make us feel happy and satisfied. Whether it's a new car, new clothes, the perfect house or the latest cell phone or computer, we are constantly encouraged to obtain things we can see and touch. Otherwise, nothing else seems to exist.

But our world is filled with things we can't actually see but nonetheless we put our trust in them every day. Our lives depend on many things that are invisible to the naked eye but that can't be touched with our hands.

Have you ever *seen* electricity? Have you ever touched air? What about gravity or love? The fact is that no one has ever *seen* electricity, air, gravity or love. They have only seen the *effects* of these things. The *effect* of electricity is light. The effect of air is our ability to breathe. The effect of gravity is that we stay attached to the earth. The effect of love is compassion and kindness.

None of these things can be seen or touched in and of themselves. Instead, they need to be discovered and used in the most positive ways possible. Electricity existed when cavemen walked the earth, but mankind hadn't yet discovered it. Only when it was discovered and understood was its power harnessed and utilized to our benefit.

Don't believe me? Then take this moment to grab a handful of air and put it into your pocket. Or look for electricity in your house, not the results of electricity like a light bulb or television working, but actual electricity. Do you have children or a friend or a pet that you love? Can you locate that love and place it on a table for a few minutes like a coin? None of these things can actually be see or touched, but we trust that they exist and use them every day.

God, in my opinion, acts in the same way as electricity, air, gravity or love. God exists and is always present, but we've only discovered one way to communicate with God—through prayer. Just because God can't be seen or touched like another human being doesn't mean the power of God can't be discovered and used to enhance our life every day.

Prayer is simply a way for us, using our minds, to speak with God, just like turning on a lamp is a way for us to benefit from the existence of electricity. As we discussed earlier, you are a spiritual being having a physical experience here on earth. But God is pure spirit (and again, without gender). So, in order to speak with God, we need to use our minds—the one part of ourselves that is most closely aligned with our spiritual nature.

Prayer is the act of direct communication, using our minds, in an effort to activate a rapport with God or Spirit. Prayer is nothing more than a pathway, or channel, that directs our thoughts and ideas towards a Higher Power with the intention of benefiting from that power. And there are many ways to pray. Let's explore a few.

9

Supplication

A common belief amongst practicing addicts is that we are the center of the universe. So many addicts and alcoholics I know, including myself, develop such an over-bloated sense of self-righteousness and self-importance that we often disregard the feelings of everyone else in our lives. Without our existence, we believe, the world would end. Life simply can't continue without us. We're that damn important!

There is a word for this called *solipsism*, a philosophical belief that the self is all that can be known and all that matters. Most addicts suffer from a ridiculous level of solipsism while engaging in self-destructive behavior that clearly contradicts their own sense of self.

I was one of the worst offenders of solipsistic ego mania. I stumbled through the world with a bloated ego and a bloated belly, demanding and craving respect, all while guzzling whiskey and inhaling cigarettes and cocaine.

By the time I got sober, I had been drinking almost daily for many years. I had reached a point in my life when I simply didn't know how to function without booze in my system. Life was just too difficult and painful, I thought, not to self-medicate. So, during the early weeks and months of my new sobriety, every single day required a herculean effort not to drink.

One of the first things I learned in the early stages of recovery was that if I was just *willing to try* to turn myself over to something bigger than my own ego, then much of the guilt and shame I felt could be lifted off of me.

It seems so contradictory that a person can despise themselves while simultaneously thinking they're the center of the universe. A sober friend of mine refers to himself as a "self-loathing narcissist", which makes me laugh every time I hear it.

I had been staggering under the crushing weight of self-loathing and solipsism for so long, that the opportunity to hand over my feelings to someone or something else was like a gift from heaven. So, I quickly memorized, and constantly repeated, one of the most well-known prayers in existence:

The Serenity Prayer
God, grant me the serenity
To accept the things I cannot change,
Courage to change the things I can,
And the wisdom to know the difference.

This simple and effective prayer of supplication gets right to the point. Most importantly, it works. I must have said this prayer twenty times per day for a year. I still recite it today on a regular basis.

A supplication prayer is the simplest and most well-known form of prayer. When we think of a child praying on her knees (or an adult alcoholic trying to rebuild his life), this is generally the type of prayer we envision. It's a way for us to ask God, or Spirit, for what we need or want.

There are many things we can ask for—guidance, mercy, awareness, good health, a home for shelter. Generally, a supplication prayer is when we ask for something for ourselves.

A prayer of supplication might be the easiest way for you to reach out to a Higher Power and ask for whatever it is *you* need.

We all go through struggles in life. Nobody, no matter how rich and successful he might be, is exempt from the "slings and arrows of outrageous fortune." But how we confront and handle the struggles that confront us can mean the difference between suffering or joy, resentment or acceptance, death or life.

Often, we are not prepared or equipped to handle life's outrageous fortunes on our own. The weight of the world becomes unbearable and we are forced to seek help outside ourselves or face defeat and possibly annihilation.

In the Lord's Prayer, Jesus tells us to ask for our "daily bread" (Mathew 6:9—13), which is more than just food. The bread or "manna" of life is the nourishment we need, not only in our stomachs, but also in our hearts and minds.

In another passage, Jesus informs us that "man shall not live on bread alone." (Matthew 4:4) This indicates that we cannot survive simply by eating food and drinking water. We must satiate our spiritual hunger by other means.

When we are spiritually hungry or our life is out of control, we can pray for what we need or want in a simple and direct way. Just ask!

You can get on your knees as a way to humble yourself, sit on your couch, lie in bed, or pray while walking. It doesn't matter. What matters is making a simple and direct request for help.

The answer or response might not arrive exactly when we want it. Often the things we seek in life take time, patience and more prayer. But the very act of prayer, the act of simply asking in a direct and humble fashion, is all that's needed to open the pathways to change.

10

Invocation

When I was learning how to pray, and learning what type of prayer worked best for me in any given situation, I often felt stuck. I didn't always know how to start.

Too often I would obsess over the right words to say or worry about how I was "supposed" to talk to God. I remembered all the fancy, flowery words I associated with prayer when I was growing up—words like "thee", "thou" and "thy". It all seemed so foreign to me, like some type of annoying Elizabethan Poetry that I had to spend hours and hours memorizing.

Since getting started was often the most difficult part of prayer for me, I found a great way to kick-start my prayers. *Invocation prayers* would get me into the right frame of mind and help me feel a connection to God. Over time, I have collected a number of invocation prayers.

Invocation prayer is like ringing a doorbell. Imagine you have something on your mind, or need help of some kind. Or, maybe you just want to feel the presence of God in your life to give you strength and comfort. So, you approach the door (your mind) that connects you to God and start ringing the doorbell through invocation prayer.

Invocation prayers are simply a way to call forth the presence and blessings of God or Spirit. This type of prayer can be especially helpful when you're feeling tired, lazy or just stuck in spiritual limbo. Invocation prayers are also ideal for group prayers because they enable everyone present to "harmonize" as a single spiritual body.

The most famous example is ***The Lord's Prayer***. Although this prayer comes to us directly from Jesus, I don't think it needs to be exclusive to Christianity.

Our Father in heaven,
Hallowed is your name.
Your kingdom come,
Your will be done,
On earth as it is in heaven.
Give us this day our daily bread,
And forgive us our trespasses,
As we forgive those who trespass against us.
And lead us not into temptation,
But deliver us from evil.

In many ways, this is the perfect prayer because it covers so much and can offer something for anyone seeking guidance, Christian or non-Christian.

The Lord's Prayer:

- Invokes God's presence as the Father to all mankind
- Praises God as the creator of everything on earth and beyond
- Asks for everything we need (bread), in both material and spiritual terms
- Asks for forgiveness and, most importantly, reminds us to be forgiving
- Concludes by asking for help in warding off evil in our lives—evil that can come from either within or outside us

Invocation prayers can be especially helpful during times of stress or fear. I know many people who recite certain prayers (or mantras) before they have to speak in public, attend a job interview, or even ask someone else out on a date (never an easy thing to do). We all have to face moments of anxiety and doubt, when we need a boost of confidence to help us step forward into the unknown abyss. An invocation prayer is often a very helpful way to call forth spiritual strength and fortitude in order to face our fears. I often recite certain prayers before business meetings or social events to boost my confidence and feel the presence of God in *every* situation I enter.

There are many invocation prayers developed over the centuries that can assist you and call forth a sense of God's presence. (In a later chapter I have included several that work for me and are easy to learn). What's important is to realize that invocation prayer is a way for you to set the spiritual tone (the "mood") as you enter into prayer. It's also a great way to either start or end your meditation.

Sometimes, simply ringing the doorbell is enough to get God's attention.

11

Unification

One of my earliest memories is being taken to a birthday party by my mother where I knew no one. I don't recall whose party it was, but I do remember the fear I experienced as soon as I arrived. I was around five or six years old at the time. My clearest memory of this event was hiding inside the house while all the other children played outside near a pool. A glass door divided me from the other kids as I watched them all playing games and swimming. Adults kept asking me why I wasn't joining in the fun, but all I could do is cry and beg them not to make me go outside. They finally gave up and left me alone until my mother returned and took me home.

Loneliness, isolation and a feeling of separation from others is something that I have struggled with my entire life. I've always felt, starting from a very early age, that I didn't belong anywhere. I was plagued with a nagging feeling that everyone else in the world understood what life was all about, and knew the secret to happiness. Even if I was at the party, I never thought

I fit in. I felt as if everyone else was part of a secret club that I wasn't allowed to join. *No entry—members only!*

I even felt this way as I grew into my adult life. I've since learned that just about everyone has felt this way at some point or another. Perhaps not everyone felt it as consistently as I did, but everyone at some point feels separated from the rest of humanity, as if they are totally alone, without a friend in the world.

The worst thing, in my opinion, is feeling separated from God or Spirit. When we feel disconnected from a Higher Source or purpose, loneliness, sadness and darkness can fill our hearts. Perhaps I wouldn't have felt so isolated and alone all those years if I had known how to connect, or unify, with life, humanity and God.

It is my deepest felt opinion that all the violence, hatred and chaos in the world can be directly linked to a disconnection from God or Spirit. And let me state clearly, religion and God are not the same thing.

Religion allows men and women to gather together in order to seek God. But that doesn't always mean we *find* God in a church, temple, synagogue or mosque. Quite often, religious leaders become so blinded by dogma, politics and power that God becomes secondary or sometimes even ignored altogether.

Religion, as we all know, has a very spotty history. A great deal of bloodshed has been spilled in the name of every major religion, Buddhism being the rare exception.

Nevertheless, I believe that religion has a very valuable place in the world. I would encourage everyone to pursue any religion that they feel comfortable with—after significant research and immersion in it. But what's most important, and crucial to any true spiritual experience, is a genuine sense of unification with a Higher Power, a feeling that you are directly connected to, and in the presence of, God. And you don't have to attend a church or temple to achieve it.

Spiritual unification has been practiced by almost every culture. Traditional Native American practices have placed an emphasis on respect for, and connection with, the Spirit of the earth and sky. The earth and the wider universe are expressed in terms of having parental powers that guide and protect us, not unlike how Christians view God as a Father to everyone and everything.

One very clear expression of unification with God and humanity comes from the Religious Science movement, most noticeably by the teachings of Ernest Holmes.

I first discovered Ernest Holmes when a friend introduced me to his book, "The Science of Mind." When I read this epic tome of spiritual wisdom, I felt like I had discovered an entirely new universe that I never knew existed. My mind was blown. I read it over and over again, as slowly as I could so I wouldn't miss a single word or idea. I was awakened to an entirely new way of thinking about my relationship with God and how I could unify with God. It was life changing.

In brief, Holmes posits that we are each a part of God's mind, separate in our individuality but part of a greater whole. Much like a drop of water can be extracted from the ocean but still be part of the ocean once it returns. All is one, all is God. When we think and use our minds, we're actually using a part of God's mind. My mind and your mind are God's mind. We are all expressions of God, not separate from God, but in fact a part of God.

This spiritual philosophy, known as Religious Science, emphasizes the "Law of Cause and Effect" that states that every action has an equal reaction. Therefore, *we manifest what we think*. Think negative thoughts, experience negative results. Think positive thoughts, experience positive results. Our happiness and destiny depend on how we train our minds. Joy and abundance are our birthright if only we can get our minds and prayers (called "treatments") aligned with God.

There's much more to the Science of Mind than my brief synopsis can offer. I encourage anyone who is interested in spiritual philosophy to read it with an open mind.

Unification prayer gives us the opportunity to feel connected with life, with humanity, with the universe. **We are all interconnected in some way. All of us carry of the same stardust. We all share the same world. We are all children of the same source of life. We all have a desire to love and be loved. We are all susceptible to loneliness and fear.**

Unification prayer allows us to realize our relationship with one another and with God. Through unification we find strength, connection, and a shared desire for a positive, fruitful life.

A Prayer for World Peace
by Ernest Holmes

I know there is but One Mind,
which is the mind of God,
in which all people live and move and have their being.
I know there is a divine pattern for
humanity and within this pattern
there is infinite harmony and peace,
cooperation, unity and mutual helpfulness.
I know that the mind of humankind,
being one with the mind of God,
shall discover the method, the way,
and the means best fitted
to permit the flow of Divine Love
between individuals and nations.
Thus harmony, peace, cooperation, unity,
and mutual helpfulness are experienced by all.
I know there will be a free interchange
of ideas, of cultures,
of spiritual concepts, of ethics, of educational systems
and scientific discoveries—for all
good belongs to all alike.
I know that, because Divine Mind has created us all,
we are bound together in one infinite and perfect unity.

I know that all people and all nations
will remain individual but unified
for the common purpose
of promoting peace, happiness,
harmony, and prosperity.
I know that deep within each person the Divine Pattern
of perfect peace is already implanted.
I now declare that in each person and
in leaders of thought everywhere
this Divine Pattern moves into action and form,
to the end that all nations and all people
will live together in peace, harmony,
and prosperity forever.

Amen. And so it is.

12

Keep It Simple

There have been times in my life when I've had a tendency to make things more complicated than necessary. There have been moments when I've ignored the easiest, most productive path to follow and instead took the most complicated and pointless path. Whether it's been choosing to remain in an unhealthy relationship, staying in a job I hate, or ignoring obvious signs of addiction, there have been many instances when I made things too complicated for my own good.

When I was first learning how to pray I did the same thing; I made it too complicated. I had this idea that prayer was supposed to be extremely mystical, with candles burning, lots of flowery language and a chorus singing in the background. My idea of prayer was like something out of a bad movie. I seriously thought that if I prayed "correctly" there would be a parting of the clouds, or a burning bush would appear in my living room and all the mysterious of the universe would be miraculously revealed to me in rush of cosmic ecstasy.

Not quite how it works, apparently.

I once asked a friend how to pray. I seriously had no idea how to go about it in a genuine, heartfelt way. What might have been obvious to others—especially to those with religious training—was a complete mystery to me.

As I've said, I had no formal religious instruction as a child. Sure, I had seen people praying in movies and on television, and I had a vague sense of what people were doing in church. But when it came to actually doing it on my own, I had no idea what was going on when people prayed.

I wondered; *Are they just babbling? Are they asking for specific things? Are they hearing voices? Who should I pray for—me or others? Should I only say nice things? Can I complain?*

My friend and I were both in the early stages of sobriety. At the time I asked him this question about prayer, he was further along the sobriety journey than I. What I had been noticing about him was the sense of peace and serenity he was beginning to express in his life. He just seemed more comfortable in the world than I felt.

After years of addiction, my instinct was still to seek comfort in a bottle. But I was determined to find another way to ease the anxiety, resentment and fear I had been struggling with my entire life. Whatever my friend was doing was something I wanted to learn how to do myself. Anything was better than continuing to feel empty and afraid.

To my shock and dismay, he showed me—right then and there! He got down on his knees and prayed out loud. I have to admit that it was an embarrassing moment for me. We were sitting in my apartment when I asked that simple question about prayer. The next thing I knew, my buddy was kneeling on the floor, talking to God.

It was weird—and certainly not something I had ever experienced in any of the bars or drug dens I had frequented. But there he was, on his knees, head bowed, hands gently clasped in front of him.

I don't remember the exact words he said, but I've tried to reconstruct the basic message he put forth. It went something like this:

Thank you, God.
Thank you for my sobriety and my life.
Thank you for giving me a chance to start over.
Thank you for your love and direction.
Please show me what I can do today
to be of service to you and to others.
Show me how I can help others who are suffering.
Help me to be loving, kind and compassionate
towards everyone on earth.
Show me what I can do today
to be the best person that I can be.
Amen.

His prayer only lasted a few moments but it seemed to cover so much.

"That's it!" he said, getting up off his knees. "It's that simple. Sometimes it goes longer, depending on how I'm feeling or what I'm dealing with. But usually it's just a moment to say thank you and ask for guidance."

What had seemed so mysterious and strange to me for so long suddenly seemed clear, simple and easy. Prayer was nothing more than a brief conversation with God or Spirit, an opportunity to express gratitude and find strength.

Kneeling is a wonderful way to humble yourself before God or whatever Higher Power you choose. Believe it or not, it actually starts to feel good to be praying on your knees, allowing yourself to let go of your ego and pride, even if it's just for a few moments. But do whatever feels best in the moment. I often pray in bed, or when I'm sitting at my desk working, or while walking, hiking or fishing.

Whether or not you pray on your knees is irrelevant. The idea is to open up a pathway to spirit by expressing thanks for what you have, asking how you can serve others, and asking for what you need. The idea is to keep it simple and always be direct.

You don't have to use flowery, biblical terminology and phrases. Just speak the way you normally speak (either silently or out loud). And, try to always express gratitude, even on days when you don't feel grateful. You'll be amazed at how powerful and life-changing gratitude in prayer can be.

13

Benefits of Prayer

Over the past twelve years, I have discovered the many benefits of prayer. Some are obvious while some are more subtle. One thing I've learned that has been crucial to my recovery and my happiness in general is that I can't control life on my own.

I need prayer in order to constantly remind myself every day that I'm not actually in charge of the universe. In fact, I'm not actually in charge of *much*— other than my own immediate actions right here, right now. Learning this fact has been one of the most liberating revelations of my life.

For so long, I thought I could control everything about life, especially the outcomes. But when things didn't turn out exactly as I planned, which was usually the case, I grew angry, frustrated and *resentful*.

I thought that if I could just get my hands gripped tightly around life's throat, I could strangle it into submission and achieve everything I wanted or thought

I deserved. Suffice it to say, this isn't how life works. Trying to control life is like trying to drink the ocean.

As time went by and I wasn't getting everything I wanted in life, the resentment compounded and I became my own walking pity party. There's an expression that states:

Resentment is like swallowing poison then waiting for the other person to die.

That's exactly how it was for me. Before I began to incorporate prayer into my daily life, I kept swallowing the poison of resentment and wondering why things never seemed to improve. I became an unpleasant person to be around and began to lose close relationships. After all, there's nothing worse than trying to be friends with an angry, bitter drunk.

It took me a very long time to learn to live life *on life's terms*, not my own. What I've come to realize is that life has its own way of working out, and it often goes in a direction I don't anticipate or expect. To quote John Lennon: "Life is what happens while you're busy making other plans."

This is a concept I've learned to embrace. Do I still make plans for the future? Yes, of course. Do I still have ambition for things I want to achieve in life? Yes, absolutely. But the key for me is to recognize that my plans, however small or grandiose, are only *ideas* about how things should turn out. I try my best in everything I do, but I leave *the results* up to God.

When I pray, it reminds me that I need to turn my will, my life and the results of my actions, over to something other than my own ego. Gratitude, no matter what the outcome might be, is the only thing I can control. So, I always try to remain thankful for what I have, while accepting what I don't have. And I remember that I'm definitely not in charge of the universe.

Benefits of prayer include:

- Communication with God or the source of life
- An opportunity to offer humility and gratitude
- A way to search for answers and direction
- A chance to align my will with God's will
- A moment to release my ego and pride
- A source of emotional and physical strength
- A time to clarify my desires and goals (whatever the outcome might be)
- A way to find motivation and inspiration
- A way to accept life on life's terms

Even a few minutes of prayer each day can yield remarkable benefits. You receive maximum benefit for minimal effort. What you get out of praying compared to what you put into it is almost hard to believe. It's like being able to go to the gym for just a few minutes every day and get in amazing physical shape. But instead of ripped abs and bulging biceps, you'll achieve something deeper and longer lasting: serenity and peace of mind.

If you can just find a few moments out of your day, every day, to express your gratitude, say thank you, and ask for guidance you will be amazed at what can transpire in your life. And your prayers don't have to be complicated or esoteric. Just pray in a simple and straight forward manner to reap the benefits. Sometimes you can pray for yourself, sometimes for others. Whoever or whatever you pray for, always have faith that there is more to your life than what you can see, hear, taste or touch. There is the unseen realm of the spirit, a spirit of love and giving that can be accessed through your mind just as electricity is accessed through a light switch.

Reach out to the unseen with simplicity and faith, let go of resentment, always knowing that your prayers will be met and that you're on a path to greater awareness and growth.

THREE

Prayer with Focus

"For prayer is nothing else than being on
terms of friendship with God."
~ Saint Teresa of Avila

"Faith and prayer are the vitamins of the soul;
man cannot live in health without them."
~ Mahalia Jackson

14

Gratitude

Of all the things to focus on when praying, gratitude is unquestionably the most important starting point. It would be easy to argue that love is the most important thing, and to a certain extent I agree. But until we are truly grateful for who we are and what we have, our ability to give and receive love is significantly blocked by ingratitude, which is the birthplace of resentment.

How can we possibly find happiness and peace, and give and receive true love, until we first acknowledge and express gratitude for the blessings we already possess?

When I first got sober, I was filled with resentment and rage. I felt that I had been cheated out of having the life I thought I deserved. I *deserved* a better life. I *deserved* more money, better friends, a healthier body. I *deserved* a beautiful wife, a large house, fame and fortune.

How could I possibly be responsible for the condition of my life? The world, and everyone in it, was to blame—not me. It was never my fault; it was all someone else's fault. Didn't the world recognize my awesomeness?

I was blinded by resentment and unable to see the part I played in my own self-destruction. I felt entitled to something better than what I had.

So, the question is this: how do we begin to focus on gratitude when we don't feel any gratitude and don't know where to find it?

It's very simple. Start with where you are right now!

Look around you. I guarantee that you will find something that you can appreciate. It can be anything. Perhaps it's the fact that you have two hands and two feet that work (assuming you do); or maybe you have a roof over your head; or maybe you have something delicious in your kitchen that you can eat later; or there's a good television show on tonight that you enjoy.

When I was new to sobriety, I used to keep a pint of Haagen Dasz coffee ice cream in my freezer at all times. My reward for staying sober each day was to eat the entire pint of ice cream at night while watching *The Office*, my favorite TV show at the time. Suffice it to say, I put on a few pounds that year.

Gaining a few pounds didn't matter. I knew I could lose the weight later. What mattered was that I had two things that I looked forward to—ice cream and my favorite show. And I was grateful for those things when I prayed in the morning and at night. It seems silly, but it worked.

If you try hard enough, you will always be able to find at least one or two things to be grateful for—a favorite pet; a good meal; a soft pillow to sleep on; a song you love; a funny joke; a good cup of coffee. Or maybe you can find gratitude in being able to help another person who is also suffering.

My friend Sheryl was struggling through the early stages of recovery and trying to piece her life back together. She didn't have any money at the time. Her personal life and health had been severely damaged by years of alcoholism and bad decisions. Like many of us who are new to sobriety, she often felt lonely and afraid. She was sad about the years she had lost to drinking and was struggling with a host or regrets and remorse. But instead of wallowing in self-pity, she started each morning with a prayer that focused on how she could help just one person that day feel better than she was feeling about herself.

So that's what she did. Every day she would look for someone who seemed sad, distressed, angry, bored or frightened. And she would approach the person (whether she knew them or not) and simply ask them "is everything okay?" Sometimes it was a person in an AA meeting. Sometimes it was just a random stranger at a coffee shop. She was surprised by how many people were willing to confide in her about how they were feeling. And more times than not, just the simple effort she made to ask them "is everything okay" seemed to have a positive effect on their mood. She also made several new friends along the way.

What Sheryl was doing was practicing gratitude by recognizing that other people were suffering too, sometimes even more than she was, and that she could help them in some small way to feel just a little better. Over time it had a huge impact on her own sense of daily gratitude and helped her cultivate a much more positive and productive outlook on life.

You don't necessarily have to go out in the street and ask strangers how they're feeling like Sheryl did. You can start with the simple things in your life. Don't focus on the negatives, only on a few things that make you smile or bring you comfort. Find the small things in life that you're grateful for and expand your outlook from there over time.

One of my favorite ways to start my prayer is to say, *Thank you for the breath in my lungs.*

A Simple Gratitude Prayer

Thank you for this day and for the breath in my lungs.
Thank you for the opportunity to start a new day.
Thank you for the chance to search
for joy and happiness.
Thank you for the opportunity to help others.

Amen.

I say this simple prayer almost every day. It seems so basic, yet it's so profound to realize that I'm breathing and alive. Sometimes it's enough to make my entire day seem brighter and more exciting.

As you grow in your daily practice, expand your list to other areas of your life for which you're grateful. Perhaps the list might include a person you meet, an interesting conversation you have, or a work of art you admire. Always be on the lookout for the things in life that bring you joy, no matter how fleeting or insignificant. Take note and use them later to start your prayer. Then say thank you.

As time goes by and you delve deeper into your practice of prayer and meditation, you will find it easier and easier to be grateful for all the gifts that life has to offer. It might take time. For me, it took several years before I was able to completely let go of all my old resentments and forgive others and myself for the wrongs of my life, real or imagined.

By practicing gratitude in our prayer and our daily lives, we are much more likely to discover acceptance, peace and serenity, which are the ultimate goals of living.

15

Love

When it comes to prayer, gratitude is the road map while love is the destination. There is no greater force in the universe than love. Without love, a mother would not feed her child. Without love, mankind would never have evolved beyond the grunting stage of cave dwellers. There would be no kindness or compassion in the world. Without love, we would have no reason to exist. Love is the nourishment that feeds our soul and illuminates our being.

Love gives life meaning. And love is not exclusive to humans—it is the universal essence permeating *all* life on earth. All creatures on earth seem to have some capacity to give and receive love. Just ask anyone who owns a dog or cat. Or, consider how primates care for one another.

Where does love come from? What is it, exactly? God is love. Love is God. It's as simple as that.

As I mentioned earlier, no one has ever *seen* love. We only see the *effects* of love. Love is something that can be felt—not something you can hold in your hand. And yet love does exist, as surely as electricity and air.

Both the gardener and the farmer know that they can't plant a tomato seed and expect to grow a cabbage. This would defy the laws of nature that we rely upon and accept. We reap what we sow. And so it is with love. When we plant seeds of love in our lives, we shall reap the rewards of what we have sown. Love begets love, just as anger begets anger and hate begets hate.

For so long, I lived on a steady diet of anger and resentment. Even going to the local coffee shop tested my state of mind. A wrong look from someone or a perceived insult (usually imagined) would fill me with contempt for human beings. It got so bad that I started to believe that people actually didn't like me, regardless of whether they knew me or not. I became paranoid and distrustful of everyone.

It saddens me to think back on how much time I wasted worrying about what others felt and thought about me, mostly because none of it was true.

As I began my recovery, I learned that in order to *receive* love, we first need to learn how to *give* love. It's not complicated, nor is it a revolutionary new idea. Mankind learned long ago that the power of love is what keeps us alive, fulfilled and happy. Without it, humans would've disappeared from earth long ago. Without love, society would collapse.

Recently, twleve boys and their soccer coach were trapped inside a cave in Thailand when a rain storm flooded their only escape route. The world looked on with horror as teams of rescuers tried to figure out how to save them from a slow and terrifying death.

People from around the world gathered together to figure out if there was any possible way to extract them from the flooded cave. After two agonizing weeks, a team of divers, engineers and Navy Seals successfully rescued all the boys at great risk to themselves. All the boys and the rescuers could have easily died during the extremely risky rescue operation.

How can this selfless act by the rescuers be anything less than a pure act of love? They put their own lives on the line in order to save a group of kids they didn't even know. Many of the rescuers had their own children waiting for them at home. Nonetheless, they found a place of courage and love within their hearts that pushed them to help others.

Everyone needs, wants and deserves love. Even our enemies (or perceived enemies) have the capacity to love and be loved. There is no creature on earth that doesn't benefit from or want love. So, when you pray, plant seeds of love in your mind that will grow in your daily life.

You can start with a simple prayer each day, asking how you can be loving towards others, a prayer like this one:

A Prayer for Love

May I be loving, kind, and giving
to everyone I encounter,
And may they find love in their life today and forever.

Sometimes we can start with the people closest to us or people we encounter during the day. This doesn't mean that we have to throw our arms around strangers and hug everyone we meet. No need to scare people.

We can, however, wish only good things for others, even strangers. We can hope that their lives are joyous and serene. We can ask silently that they have lives filled with love and friendship. Even if we don't feel these things for ourselves yet, we must try to project loving kindness onto others.

Doing so may not change the world overnight—but it will adjust your mind. You'll start to see people differently. You'll feel more empathy and compassion for others. And in return, others will begin to feel the energy you are putting out and return back to you the seeds you have sown.

16

Compassion

n order to love and be loved, we must nurture a
desire and willingness to be compassionate toward
all living beings. If we want to align ourselves with
God or Spirit, it's important that we express empathy
for others and always do our best to be helpful to anyone that needs our help.

When I was a young boy, there was a strange-look-
ing, partially-blind man who lived in our small town. As
children, we were scared of him. He was an odd-look-
ing fellow with disheveled clothing and scraggly hair.
And, he often strolled slowly through town with a long
walking stick swinging in front of him to navigate the
sidewalk.

Whenever I saw him approaching, I would cross
to the other side of the street. Along with the other
children, I made fun of him and often taunted him
with cruel words and snickers. Instead of helping him
by opening a door or just saying hello, we made fun of
him.

One day I was in the car with my mom. I was around ten years old at the time. We were driving toward our apartment when we spotted the weird blind man, wandering near our home. Apparently, he had accidentally walked down our street and was lost. He looked confused, uncertain of which way to go.

I can't tell you how shocked I was when my mother pulled our car over to the side of the road AND ASKED IF HE WANTED A RIDE! For the record, my mother was, and is, one of the kindest, most compassionate people I have ever known. She has always gone out of her way to help others.

When this strange creature said yes and got into our car, I was overwhelmed with anxiety and fear. The idea of letting this weirdo into our car was too much for my young mind to handle. I sat in the back seat and stared at the back of his head and his matted hair. I didn't say a word while he and my mom engaged in innocuous pleasantries about the weather.

Finally, we got him to where he needed to go and started heading back home.

"Why did you let him in our car?" I demanded to know.

"Because he needed our help," my mother said. "He was lost. He's a nice man. He can't see very well, that's all. You don't need to be afraid of him."

To my mother, it was just that simple. When someone needs help, you give it to them.

That was many years ago but I still remember that day so clearly. It was one of the first significant lessons I learned about compassion. There's nothing complicated or frightening about it. We simply help others whenever we can. And if we can't help them directly, the very least we can do is sympathize with their struggles and pain.

The key is to begin to see ourselves in others and recognize our shared humanity. Then, we are much more likely to be motivated to do our best to be of service and help others in any way we can.

This holds true for other beings that inhabit the earth as well. I'm not advocating for veganism, but it's important that we act as good stewards of the planet and always show kindness and compassion to *all* living creatures, not just people. I believe that most animals have a high capacity to feel pain, sadness and loss. Therefore, we need to recognize their unique spiritual identity as much as possible, through kindness and respect.

We all face difficulties in life. It's part of being human. But it's important that we try to see ourselves in others and recognize the things that we share as people, not the differences. When others are suffering, we can stop for a moment amidst the chaos of our busy lives and say this simple prayer:

A Prayer of Compassion

There, but for the grace of God, go I.
Today may I be kind and compassionate
to everyone I meet.

May I be of service to others who need my help.
And may I show respect and love
towards all beings on earth.

Amen.

17

Humility

Pride can be both a blessing and a curse. It's healthy to feel proud about who you are as a human being and a child of God. It's good to feel a sense of pride about certain things in life like being a good husband or wife, father or mother, son or daughter. We should take pride in hard work and living a life that is honest and charitable. But it's also easy to develop a bloated sense of ego that can grow into arrogance and know-it-all-ism.

This is true for both addicts and non-addicts. Pride is like a balloon that we fill with our own sense of self-worth. But if we continuously fill the balloon with hubris and conceit, eventually it will burst. Then we'll be forced to pick up the tatters of our identity in order to rediscover who we are and how we can serve others instead of only our own ego. It can be a difficult and humbling experience to accept humility as a part of our life.

First and foremost, let's be clear: humility is NOT the same as humiliation. It surprises me how often people get these two words confused. We are not trying to seek humiliation. Life is difficult enough already without feeling embarrassment or shame. (I have experienced plenty of both in my life and I know that I don't need any more. I'm sure that you don't either.)

What I'm talking about is humility—a willingness to:

- Feel humble and grateful
- Accept that we are sometimes powerless against the storms of life
- Understand that we can nevertheless remain content and serene

The sooner we admit that we are powerless and God is in charge, the faster we will find comfort and peace. Humility is our opportunity to accept life on life's terms, not our own.

Sometimes the best thing we can do for ourselves is to simply LET GO. It's amazing how liberating it can feel to say, "I'm not in charge of the universe, so right now I'm just going to let go of all my worries and fears and let life take over."

The world continues to turn every day. The forces of nature never cease. The sun rises and the sun sets. The universe is incomprehensibly vast—so vast and ever-changing that mankind has virtually no input, no control over any of it.

We are not in charge of much of anything. God is in charge—and realizing this is a gift. We are here for the ride, so enjoy the passing scenery.

Some people might think this sounds nihilistic or depressing. But to me, it's the most joyous discovery I have ever made. The first time I tried to let go and humble myself before God and the universe, I felt a tremendous weight come off my shoulders. To admit that I wasn't in charge of life or its outcomes allowed me to stop the daily struggle of trying to force life to be what I thought it *should* be.

Instead, I learned that life is spontaneous, always surprising and different every day. There are forces in the world that are far greater than our own needs and wants. It doesn't matter *what* I want or think I deserve. What matters is being prepared for every event that comes my way, good or bad, and accepting the outcome.

When I think of trying to force life into submission, I'm reminded of the terror I used to feel any time I had to speak in public. Most people share this fear. Due to my fear of public speaking, I went to great lengths to avoid it, trying to control any situation that might trigger that fear.

As a student in high school and college, for example, I always took an "F" grade when it came to giving oral reports. I simply refused to do it because I was so afraid to speak in front of my peers.

Then when I was newly sober, I had the opportunity to speak in front of many people about my experience as an alcoholic. At first, I was so nervous I could barely open my mouth. But sharing our story is a big part of recovery. I knew I had to try if I wanted to stay clean.

Other people taught me that it didn't matter *how* I felt about speaking in public. Staying sober is a life-and-death situation for many people. And, the people listening to me were trying to stay alive. My silly little fears meant nothing compared to their survival. My fear was irrelevant. The only thing that mattered was sharing a message of hope and strength so that *others* might stay sober.

This was an incredibly humbling message to receive and one I took to heart. It made speaking in public easier and easier as time went by.

I learned that helping others is a very good way to achieve and maintain a healthy sense of humility. Acknowledging the grace that we've been given in our lives is another. Instead of wailing and punching against the injustices of life, we can take a moment each day to humble ourselves before God or Spirit, rejoicing in our humility and allowing ourselves to live life on life's terms, not our own. It might be the most liberating experience you ever discover.

The 7th Step Prayer

*My creator, I am now willing
that you should have all of me, good and bad.
I pray that you now remove from me
every single defect of character*

*which stands in the way of my usefulness
to you and to my fellows.
Grant me strength as I go out from
here to do your bidding.*

Amen.

18

Service

There have been many times in my life when I spent so much time obsessing over how I was *feeling* that I forgot to focus on things I could actually be *doing*.

"Navel gazing" is defined as self-indulgent or excessive contemplation of oneself or a single issue, at the expense of a wider view. This is a concept I know all too well. I'm guilty of spending far too much time over-thinking and obsessing about things that really aren't that important, usually things about myself that no one in their right mind would really care about.

Too often we become trapped in a never-ending cycle of inner reflection and self-analysis. This can easily devolve into self-obsession and selfishness. Another way to put it is "analysis paralysis," the phenomenon of spending so much time analyzing ourselves that we become spiritually paralyzed. It's very easy to allow ourselves to wallow in self-reflection, whether we're thinking about how sad we are (*"woe-is-me-ism"*) or how great we are (*"damn-I'm-awesome-ism"*).

Not that inner reflection is always a bad thing. In fact, it can be an important part of healing and recovery from many things, including addiction or heartbreak. But we need to be careful not to get stuck in our inner-world. Otherwise, we face the danger of becoming isolated and separated from the outer-world.

We should always do our best to look outward, beyond our own self, to the world around us. The easiest way to do this is to seek opportunities to make ourselves available to serve others. Service gets us out of our own heads and focuses our attention away from ourselves.

If you can simply start each day with the question, "How can I be of service to others today?" you'll be amazed by the number of service opportunities that appear in your daily life. Just putting the question out there is enough to spark an acute awareness of those around you who might be in distress.

You don't have to save the world or cure cancer. Typically, it's just a matter of showing a small kindness—perhaps talking to someone who feels sad or lonely, offering a genuine compliment, or giving a ride to someone who doesn't own a car. There are countless ways we can be of service to others every day, and by simply stating it in prayer, the opportunities will present themselves.

I know a man who spent twenty-five years in prison for armed robbery. I'll call him William. He is a scary-looking dude, with 250 pounds of solid muscle! His arms are like tree trunks. He's covered in tattoos, including on his neck and face. After spending the majority of his life behind bars, he is quiet and appears incredibly menacing.

Most people who encounter him for the first time instinctively step aside and lower their eyes, in deference to his alarming appearance. William is clearly not a man you want to mess with—and yet he is one of the gentlest, kindest men I have ever known.

I met William in a 12-step meeting. Over time we got to know each other, talking and joking before and after each meeting. One of the things that fascinated me the most about William (aside from his vast experience in the penal system) was his friendship with a tiny, frail old lady who also attended our meeting.

I'll call her Betty. If you saw her next to you at a restaurant, you'd see someone who looks like a sweet little grandmother. Betty was around 75 years old and recovering from a nasty addiction to crack cocaine and heroin. She had trouble walking and needed assistance getting up and down from her chair.

Every day, William drove his beat-up car to Betty's house, picked her up and drove her to our meeting. He always got out of the car first, walked around to the passenger side, opened the door for her, and helped her out. Once they got into the meeting, he made sure that she had a seat next to her friends before he went to find a seat for himself. After the meeting, he'd escort her out and help her back into his car. Then he drove her home.

They often laughed together, sharing their own inside stories and jokes. It was a strange and beautiful friendship, and one that has always inspired me. Every time I think of William and Betty, I smile.

We can all learn from William. Here is a man whom you might expect to be bitter and angry about the experiences of his life. Instead he is selfless and giving, being of service to someone who needed his help. Service gives his life purpose, helps him stay sober, and enriches his life with an unlikely friendship.

The Prayer of St. Francis of Assisi

Lord, make me an instrument of your peace:
Where there is hatred, let me sow love;
Where there is injury, pardon;
Where there is doubt, faith;
Where there is despair, hope;
Where there is darkness, light;
Where there is sadness, joy.
God, grant that I may not so much seek
To be consoled as to console,
To be understood as to understand,
To be loved as to love.
For it is in giving that we receive,
It is in pardoning that we are pardoned,
And it is in dying that we are born to eternal life.

Amen.

19

Clarity

L ife can be very chaotic and unpredictable. How often do we start our day with a specific plan in mind, only to see that plan dissolve completely as we're bombarded by a series of unexpected situations and events that are beyond our control? This can happen in a single day or across many years.

Perhaps we had plans for the trajectory of our life, for how things were supposed to turn out. When we're young, most of us spend a great deal of time thinking and planning for our future. Then, as time passes, those plans and ideas take on new shapes and go in new directions, often altering our original plans beyond recognition.

Life has a way of taking us in directions we don't always anticipate or even want. In times of unexpected change, we can easily become frustrated and confused, doubting our ability to stay focused and alert. Our minds can become clouded by self-doubt, anger and depression. We can become mentally fatigued if we constantly have to adjust our plans and hopes.

At times like these, it's easy to lose our sense of purpose and direction. Praying for clarity of mind is a powerful way to stay in the moment. It helps us learn how to maintain a sense of purpose and hope, even when we're sucker-punched by chaos.

When my father was in the final stages of cancer, I put my small business on hold and moved to San Francisco where he was living, so I could help my brothers attend to him. In addition to dad's cancer, our stepmother was showing the early stages of dementia. So, instead of helping just one parent, we had to deal with the complexities of two sick parents.

This was one of the most difficult and heartbreaking periods of my life, to put it mildly. Every single day required enormous amounts of patience and fortitude. We had to deal with round-the-clock concerns about care, doctors, nurses, meals, medicine, sleep and hospice.

No day was the same. We never knew what to expect or how we were going to deal with whatever came next. It was an unbelievably exhausting situation. But our love for our father and stepmother kept us fighting through every trial that confronted us each day.

Prayer was crucial to keeping my sanity—often hourly prayer. I constantly prayed for clarity of purpose. I began every morning asking for help in keeping a clear mind so that I could maintain my strength and be of service to my sick parents and my brothers. And I prayed throughout each day, often slipping off to a quiet room or stepping outside just to have a moment to pray in peace.

It would have been so easy to give up by giving in to sadness and depression. But I knew that if I gave up, I couldn't provide the help I needed to give. My family needed me to be completely present. What good was I going to be if I became overwhelmed and curled up into a ball of self-pity?

So, I prayed around the clock for clarity of mind and purpose.

There was nothing easy about the experience. We stayed with dad for several months until he finally passed. Then we took the necessary steps to address our stepmother's dementia. Yet through it all, I managed to maintain my composure and strength more than I ever would have thought possible.

Granted, I had a few breakdowns along the way when I became overwhelmed with sadness and emotion. But I was able to cry my way through each of these occurrences and find new strength, even at the lowest points. And I credit prayer with giving me the strength I needed to get through each day, no matter what life threw at me.

During times of extreme difficulty, upheaval or sudden change, we need to keep our mind clear so that we can focus on what is most important. When we are overwhelmed by change or emotional stress, it's easy for our mind to become clouded by fear and doubt. Our thought shuts down and we have difficulty making clear, rational decisions about what is best for ourselves and others.

By praying for clarity, we can often clear away much of the confusion in our head and see what is most important and how to approach each stressful situation that appears with calmness and foresight.

A Prayer for Clarity and Purpose

Lord, bless me with clarity of mind
to see what is important.
Help me to stay focused and to remember
the things that bring me happiness and joy.
No matter what comes my way today,
help me to see my role in your plan,
So that I might help others and find my purpose.

Amen.

20

Right Action

can't begin to list all of the bad decisions I've made in my life. There are far too many to remember. And I'm not just talking about bad decisions related to addiction, which are countless. I'm also talking about the simple day-to-day decisions throughout my life that have created problems, stress and anxiety.

Whether it's as simple as deciding on the right food to eat for breakfast or as complex as choosing the right career path, we have to make decisions every day. And those decisions impact our lives, as well as the lives of those we love. Sometimes we make the correct decisions, other times we don't. It's important to find a way to make correct, positive and healthy decisions every day.

Praying for right action is a great opportunity to set ourselves on a positive path for the day. This way, we become conscious of every decision we make—hopefully decisions that will deliver a positive outcome.

For many years I worked as a freelance marketing consultant, helping small business owners market and promote their companies. Most of the time I would bill the client every 30 days, then wait a few weeks to receive payment while I continued working for them. Getting paid usually wasn't an issue since most of the companies I worked for were well established with big budgets. However, I once had a particular client who, apparently, didn't have any money to pay me for my work even though we had signed a contract.

They were nice people, or so it seemed, and I was getting their company a lot of exposure. However, every time I sent them an invoice at the end of each 30 day billing cycle, they suddenly went quiet and I had difficulty tracking them down. I would call and email them with polite requests for payment. They would either fail to respond or tell me that they were "working on it" and would send me the payment "in the next few days."

I accepted their excuses for a while but after 90 days of not being paid (and accumulating a very large debt that they owed me), I grew anxious. I was living on a budget and every dollar counted in order to keep my business and my life financially afloat. Eventually, as time passed, my requests for payment became less polite, instead growing angrier and more hostile.

Nonetheless, the client continued to promise payment, telling me that they were just waiting for a new round of financing to come through. Despite their assurances, payment never came.

My anxiety grew into full-fledged panic. I began a campaign to demand my money, sending threatening emails and leaving furious voicemails. I admit that this was not a particularly Zen way to approach the situation. In fact, it was the *exact opposite* of Zen.

I was growing increasingly enraged. I couldn't sleep. I developed stomach pains and headaches from the stress. I harbored intense resentment towards the company and its owners. I created revenge scenarios in my head. At one point I decided I was going to take legal action and sue them.

I spoke with a friend who had experience in this sort of thing. He informed me that it was going to take a very long time to bring the case to court. He also said that it was unlikely that I was going to get paid anyway, since the company was broke. I was going to spend months or perhaps years chasing after money that I would probably never receive, all the while spending my own money on legal fees.

The same friend who gave me this advice suggested, very gently, that perhaps I would be best served if I just "let this one go". What was the point in chasing after something that might never materialize?

I was going insane from the anger and frustration. I needed the money, but I also knew that the stress was becoming too much to bear.

After a great deal of thought and prayer, I made the decision to just let it go and forget about the money I was owed.

This might sound like a foolish decision. But the fact is, once I made this decision I *immediately* felt like the weight of the world had fallen from my shoulders. I started to relax. The tension in my body eased. I was able to sleep peacefully. The stomach problems and headaches faded away. My appetite returned. By simply making the decision to choose my health and peace of mind over monetary rewards—regardless of whether the money was due to me or not—had an instant and positive impact on me.

And, to top it off, I said a prayer for the business owners, wishing that they find success and peace in their lives, no matter what. I had to let go of my resentment. The best way to do that was to simply say a prayer for those who had done me wrong.

I was free.

I'm not suggesting that you just ignore or discard anyone who wrongs you. But it's important to know when it is appropriate to make a decision in favor of your own sanity. Depending upon the circumstances, that might mean letting go of a bad financial situation or something else that is negatively affecting your life. The decisions we make each day have an impact on our health and our future. If we can focus our prayers on right action, we stand a much better chance of making correct decisions.

A Prayer for Right Action

God, help me to make the right decisions today.
Help me to take the right action in
every encounter and situation.

THE SOBER JOURNEY

May I think clearly before I proceed
in every moment of the day.
And may my actions bring positive
results for me and for others.

Amen.

21

Health

When I was still drinking I had a weekend routine that went something like this: drink all night Friday into the morning hours. Sleep until noon or later then get up and drink three or four cups of coffee. Sit on the couch all day watching television and eating cheeseburgers, French fries, burritos and milk shakes; the greasier the food the better. While stuffing my face, I would sit there feeling sorry for myself and wondering why my life wasn't better than it should be. The world owed me a life better than this, damn it. Then around four o'clock I'd crack my first beer and start the cycle all over again. Suffice it to say, I gained a lot of weights and developed a number of health problems after a few years of this lifestyle.

Remember the old saying, "*An apple a day keeps the doctor away*"? It may seem quaint and silly, but there is some truth to this timeless proverb. What we put into our bodies each day, the food we consume, has a direct impact on both our short-term and long-term health.

Which is healthier—eating fruits and vegetables every day or eating donuts and ice cream every day? I promise, if you live on nothing but donuts, ice cream and other junk food, no matter how delicious they might be in the moment, you're going to suffer from serious health issues. But if you make a commitment to consume fresh, natural foods you will reap the benefits by nurturing a healthy body.

Just as we need to feed our body healthy food, we also need to feed our mind and spirit with positive energy. This positive energy can be accessed by praying for good health.

But what does good health mean? In my opinion, good health starts on the inside. Good health involves:

- A positive attitude
- A joy for life
- Seeing the best in others
- Ridding ourselves of resentment and envy
- A desire to grow and learn
- Developing compassion
- Loving ourselves
- Having gratitude

One of my favorite expressions is, "*As within, so without.*" How we feel on the inside will always affect how we feel and behave on the outside. Positive energy flows through us like clean, clear water, nourishing every aspect of our mind, spirit and soul.

According to the Mayo Clinic, the benefits of a positive attitude include:

- Increased life span
- Lower rates of depression
- Lower levels of distress
- Greater resistance to the common cold
- Better psychological and physical well-being
- Better cardiovascular health and reduced risk of death from cardiovascular disease
- Better coping skills during hardships and times of stress

One of the easiest ways to start is to replace resentment with gratitude. When we pray, we can simply list all the things we're grateful about in our life. Or we can pray by giving thanks for the things we enjoy or find beautiful.

During the early days of my recovery from alcohol, I slowly began to recognize how much anger, fear and resentment had accumulated in me over the years. I was pissed off at the world and everyone in it. I chose to consume the poisonous junk food of anger and resentment rather than feed my body and mind with the nourishing benefits of hope and gratitude. I was rotting from the inside and it showed in my attitude and outlook on life. I didn't want to address these issues because they were too painful to confront.

I made it a point to start praying for a better attitude and a willingness to appreciate what I had—not what I had lost. I began to incorporate hope and gratitude into my daily prayer. It wasn't easy at first. I had been sick and angry for so long that I'd forgotten how to feel good.

It sounds ridiculous now, but at the time I couldn't remember how it felt to be optimistic and excited about *anything*. I was buried in the depths of depression and fear and needed to find a way out of the hole I had dug.

Slowly, over time, my prayers began to take on a new shape and color. Every day I asked for a healthy body and mind. I listed all the things in my life that were good and I accepted any challenges I was facing instead of trying to bury them. Most importantly, *I developed gratitude and rejected resentment in any form.*

It is amazing how much this helped me recover. I started to feel better. I began to smile more. My sleep improved, my depression lifted, and I began to trust people more. I began the process of forgiving myself and others.

Praying for good health is one of the most important things we can do for ourselves. It can have an immediate and long-term impact on every aspect of our life, body, mind and soul.

A Prayer for Good Health

Thank you, God, for my life.
Thank you for this day.
Thank you for my family and friends.
Thank you for the breath in my lungs.
Thank you for my health and well-being.
Thank you for the beauty in nature.
Thank you for the opportunity to serve others.
May I be a blessing to everyone I meet today.

Amen.

22

Success

Everyone has their own definition of the word "success." It can be applied to so many situations that it becomes difficult to define. Too often we think of success only in terms of financial net worth or earning power. The size of someone's bank account or house is often the way we determine whether or not someone is successful.

This is a very narrow view of success and focuses only on one aspect of a person's life (I will address material wealth later on). In actuality our lives are much too complex and layered for our net worth or earning power to be the barometer of whether or not we are successful.

Is a single mother who raises healthy, well-adjusted children entirely on her own less successful than a man who runs a Fortune 500 company? Is a teenage boy who joyfully participates in the Special Olympics less successful than a college student who gets drafted into the NFL? Is a heroin addict who gets clean and then goes on to earn a degree in social work less successful than a person who gets elected to the U.S. senate?

The famous basketball star, Julius "Dr. J" Erving once said: "The key to success is to keep growing in all areas of life—mental, emotional, and spiritual, as well as physical."

If we take a different view of the word "success," we'll realize that it's a relative term that can be applied to so many different situations in life.

I worked in the corporate world for many years. At one point I held a management position with a large company where I earned a substantial income. I drove a flashy, expensive car, traveled often, and received a fat paycheck and large quarterly bonuses. In conventional terms, I was on a successful career track with a bright future ahead of me.

However, while I was receiving all these financial rewards, I was struggling with depression, alcoholism and drug addiction. Emotionally and spiritually I was completely empty and had lost all sense of meaning in my life.

Eventually I lost the fancy job, the car and the money. All the material success was gone and I was left with just me (*Yikes!*). The final descent to rock bottom had begun and it was several years before I completed my fall into addiction, followed by recovery.

I had to start my life over again, almost like being reborn. Early recovery is about picking up the pieces of our life and trying to assemble it back together in a way that is productive, healthy and successful.

Success for me, in early recovery, was first measured by not drinking, one day at a time. Every day that became my goal. And to make it through an entire day without taking a drink was a successful day. This is no easy feat, as any alcoholic will agree. Once you've become fully dependent on any substance that provides a daily escape from fear and elevates your emotions, it can seem impossible to live without it. It took quite a while to get used to not having my daily comfort from a bottle. But I kept at until one day I realized that I was actually able to go without a drink; the obsession had been lifted.

Then over time I incorporated new goals for success: improving my physical health, learning how to help others with their addictions, and eventually, starting my own business.

Over the years, I've had so many types of success on so many different levels that it's hard to keep track. Of course, I've had many setbacks as well, but I never, *ever* use the term "failure" because it carries negative energy. I don't need or want negativity in my life.

I learned early on that praying for success doesn't necessarily mean asking for financial rewards. Instead it means asking for personal excellence in every part of my life. For me, success is often measured by how good a husband I am, how good a son I am, how good a brother I am, or whether or not I'm able to help someone that day. Simply being kind is a form of success.

When I work, I want to give it everything I have, without worrying about the results or financial reward.

When I go to bed at night, I want to know that I lived a full life that day and did as many things as I could to learn and grow. When I go to sleep, I want to know that I tried my best every minute of the day, no matter how things turned out. That is success.

However you define success, make sure to start with simple goals that improve your health and quality of life. You can have lots of money, but if you're making bad choices, or are always sick or depressed, all the money in the world won't alleviate your suffering. Your spiritual health has to come first if you truly want to experience what real success feels like.

A Prayer for Success

God, today may I be successful in everything that I do.
May I be the best that I can be.
May I always be kind to others and to myself.
May I be kind and compassionate
toward every living being.
May I work hard and not worry about the results.
May I live life on life's terms and be filled with joy,
knowing that I tried my best every step of the way.

Amen.

23

Spiritual Wealth

The word "wealth," like "success," is a relative term that can be applied to many different things. Financial wealth is the most obvious and common way to use the word. But often our spiritual bank account feels empty. We become emotionally impoverished to the point that we can become depressed and frustrated by life, with all of its challenges.

For some people this inner bankruptcy leads to addiction, self-abuse, isolation and in extreme cases even suicide. But we have access to an abundance of spiritual riches that can be accessed through prayer and meditation.

Material wealth is nothing to be ashamed of, nor do I believe that there is anything intrinsically wrong with, or sinful about, money or financial wealth (I will explore this more in the next chapter). Money is just another form of energy—a means by which we can obtain and exchange goods and labor and enjoy some of the luxuries that the world offers. It is neither good nor bad.

However, to seek happiness from money *alone* is always futile. No matter how much money we have, if we're sad or depressed on the inside, a new house, car or shiny piece of jewelry won't ease our suffering. Not for more than an hour or at most, a day, anyway. It's a temporary fix when what we really need is long lasting, deeply-felt spiritual fulfillment.

The obvious question then is: what is spiritual wealth? Many of us would agree that spiritual wealth includes:

- Feeling unified with God or Spirit
- Feeling connected to all life on earth
- Recognizing our value as human beings
- Feeling serene, even in times of turmoil
- Feeling calm, even in times of chaos
- Our capacity to feel joy at being alive
- Feeling gratitude for our blessings
- Love for ourselves and others

The list could go on much longer. You can certainly add your own ideas of what spiritual wealth means to you. But the point to remember is that while material wealth can solve certain types of problems, it is *spiritual* wealth that gives life meaning and purpose.

When I turned forty, I was at a point in my life when I felt dead inside. My capacity to feel much of anything was almost nonexistent. The only way I was able to feel anything was by getting drunk. (It's not called *spirits in a bottle* for nothing!) And even getting drunk wasn't working very well anymore. I was at a point where the more I drank, the worse I felt, but at least I was feeling *something*. That's how I rationalized it.

I was spiritually empty inside. I had lost my ability to appreciate the things in life that had once brought me joy. Family, friends, travel, work, music…nothing held any interest for me anymore.

It wasn't until I got sober three years later at age 43 that I finally began to feel alive again. In fact, in that first year of being newly sober, I was bombarded by *FEELINGS* (the dreaded "F" word!). Feelings are one of the first things we encounter once we remove the numbing agents we've been ingesting for so long. Alcohol and drugs are highly effective at blocking our emotions. So once these blockers are removed we're left to face the churning sea of emotions and *feelings* that have been trapped inside us for so long. It can be startling and overwhelming to many people who are newly sober. In fact, it's these intense feelings that often cause relapse because they're just too much to handle for some people.

I experienced these intense waves of emotion with dread and sometimes panic. I really had no idea this was what sobriety was about when I started. I was an emotional wreck for quite a while, often crying and lashing out irrationally. But over time I was able to control my emotions through a combination of step work, prayer and meditation. Eventually I learned how to experience good feelings like joy and gratitude once again. It took time, but eventually I reached a point where I was happy more often than not.

My fiftieth birthday, seven years later, was one of the best days of my life. Fifty is an age many people fear. But for me it was a great achievement, a wonderful milestone—and not only in terms of my recovery, either. The fact that I was still alive was a miracle in and of itself. Better still was the fact that I was very content with my life.

I'm not claiming that my life was, or is, perfect in any way. There's no such thing as perfect. But I had achieved a level of serenity and acceptance that I never would have thought possible when I was forty. I was seven years clean and sober, married to my amazing wife, and we had adopted a beautiful dog. I had a home in Lake Tahoe, and I was surrounded by family and friends who loved me just as I loved them.

What could be better? Everything I had ever wanted was with me and within me. I wasn't financially wealthy, but I was content and happy and I felt intense joy in just being alive. Most importantly, I had given up my fight against life. I was simply enjoying the ride, living life on life's terms. Spiritually, I felt like the wealthiest man alive.

Today I am fifty-four and, on most days, I still have that same feeling of spiritual contentment. I pray daily that it stays this way.

A Prayer for Spiritual Wealth

Lord, bless me with peace, serenity and joy today.
May I always recognize my blessings.
May I face each day with gratitude.
May I meet every challenge with hope.
May I always bring love, compassion
and kindness into the world.

Amen.

24

Material Wealth

Too often we feel guilty or uncomfortable with the idea of pursuing material wealth while attempting to achieve spiritual wealth. Some people believe that the two goals are mutually exclusive and can't (or shouldn't) be achieved or pursued at the same time. The idea is that a spiritual life is somehow contaminated or corrupted if we also desire money and material "stuff" like houses and nice cars.

As I stated earlier, I believe that seeking happiness from money *alone* is futile. However, I also recognize that human beings have a deep longing to own and enjoy beautiful things. We see and feel value in owning our own home, and by being able to get from place to place in a safe and comfortable vehicle. We also have a deep desire to provide for, and protect, the people we love which often requires a safe home in a safe neighborhood, clothing, healthy food, education and medical care, all of which cost money.

Mankind has been attracted to gold, diamonds and sparkly things since the dawn of time. We are hunter-gatherers by instinct and by evolution. This aspect of our humanity has been essential in allowing us to survive and thrive on earth. It is an undeniable part of our life on earth and to ignore this fact is foolish and naïve.

We are interested in "stuff" and enjoy getting new stuff whenever we can. One of my favorite comedians, George Carlin, said it best: "A house is just a place to keep your stuff while you go and get more stuff."

It's as simple as that. We shouldn't overthink it. There should be no shame in owning anything, as long as it's acquired honestly and without harming others. In fact, having money in the bank and a roof over our head allows us more time to pursue our spiritual needs. Unless you want to try living alone in a cave in the desert, surviving on nothing but locust and honey, you're going to need to earn an honest living without shame or guilt. For me, I like meditating on my nice comfortable couch in my nice comfortable house, and I want it to stay that way.

Of course, the pursuit of material acquisition can be taken to the extreme. Many people put the pursuit of money and material wealth above everything else, including family, friendship and faith. Indeed, for many people, money is its own form of religion and it dominates their lives.

Again, I believe that seeking happiness from money alone is usually futile and even dangerous. But money is nothing more than a form of energy that we can exchange for goods or services. It's neither inherently good nor bad. But in our society, it is certainly necessary. So, we should learn to embrace and enjoy it for what it is, without fear or contempt.

I moved to Los Angeles soon after college. At the time, it felt like I had moved to heaven. As a young man, there was no place else I wanted to be. I had a wonderful time there for the first few years. Los Angeles can be an amazing place, especially when you're young and exploring life. It's filled with beautiful people, movie stars and amazing restaurants and night clubs.

It is also incredibly expensive to live comfortably and well in Los Angeles and the opportunities for self-destruction are abundant (trust me). Eventually I grew tired of Los Angeles and wanted (and needed) to move. I wasn't young anymore and had grown into a full-fledged alcoholic who was financially broke.

I had begun dreaming of moving to the mountains, Lake Tahoe in particular. I had always found peace and joy in the wilderness, and was ready to exchange my city life for mountain life. But I had no money to speak of, which meant that I was unable to plan my escape. So, I put the dream aside and accepted that I was stuck in the City of Angels (and *devils!*).

Later, after I managed to put together a couple of years of sobriety, the dream of moving to the mountains resurfaced. At the time, I was working freelance jobs in public relations. I wasn't making much money, just enough to get by. But I began to pray that someday

I'd be able to land a contract that was big enough that I could finally make the move to Lake Tahoe.

It didn't happen overnight. But the more I prayed and the harder I worked, the bigger the contracts I kept getting. I prayed for new clients. I prayed for more income. I prayed to one day achieve what I so desperately wanted. I was constantly putting positivity and hope into my prayers and into my mind, focusing on manifesting the things I wanted and needed.

Finally, I landed my biggest account ever. I had a very specific amount of money that I needed to have in order to transition out of Los Angeles without worry. The contract I landed was exactly the amount I needed to move. Six weeks later I was living in a beautiful apartment in the mountains, right next to the shores of Lake Tahoe.

That was one of the happiest times of my life and one of the best decisions I ever made. But it couldn't have happened without recognizing that I needed money to make the transition. The money I earned helped change my life for the better, and to this day I still thank God for blessing me with the material wealth I needed and had asked for through prayer.

A Prayer for Financial Abundance

*God, bless me with financial prosperity and abundance.
Help me to achieve wealth enough for
a home, security and comfort.*

THE SOBER JOURNEY

May I succeed and grow in every part of my life.
May I always be generous and giving
with all that I have been given.
May I always be charitable to those in need.
May I always respect and enjoy all my blessings.

Amen.

25

Serenity

Having a calm, peaceful mind is something that eluded me for most of my life until I learned how to pray and meditate. Before I got sober, I led a lifestyle that was chaotic at best and dangerous at worst. The idea of tranquility—if I even considered such a thing—was a joke. I lived a fast life, filled with intoxicants, cheap thrills and pointless pursuits. There was very little meaning to my existence, as far as I could discern.

For many years I drove headlong into a blinding blizzard of bad decisions, heartbreaking relationships and reckless behavior. By the time I reached the end of that stage of my life, I was left dazed and bewildered. My spirit was crushed and my mind was in tatters. I don't mean to sound melodramatic when I describe how I felt right before I finally broke free from decades of addiction. But the truth is that I was like a man who had been skinned alive in the middle of a sandstorm. I was beat-up, raw and frightened. I wanted only one thing…

Peace of mind.

I hadn't felt peace in so long that I had forgotten what it felt like. My mind was swirling with shame, regret, resentment, sadness and anger. I was stuck with only my own thoughts—and they weren't good. My mind was telling me that I was a horrible person, worthless and undeserving of redemption or grace.

It's amazing how much we beat ourselves up. Not everyone takes it to the extreme that I did (I hope not, anyway.) But most of us at times allow ourselves to become mentally unsettled and self-critical, to the point where we can become depressed and angry.

It's important that we take a few moments each day to try to calm our minds and soothe our hearts. We do this by reminding ourselves that we're not perfect and don't have to be. We are human and we make mistakes. We make bad decisions sometimes, but regret does us no good. We hurt ourselves and sometimes other people, but we can always make things right. Every hour and every day presents a new opportunity to correct the errors of our past and move forward in our lives, free from shame or sorrow.

Serenity is one of the most important gifts we have at our disposal. It is readily available to us if we're willing to take a few simple steps, beginning with prayer. Serenity has been proven to:

- Help us to make better decisions
- Clear our minds of regret and anger
- Release resentment

- Help us stay calm in most situations
- Dissolve sorrow and remorse
- Make us more enjoyable and approachable
- Help us sleep better
- Open the channels to God or Spirit

Achieving complete serenity might not be possible for everyone, but it's important to try. We all have bad days when we wake up in a funk and there is nothing that we can do to improve our mood. But that's okay, too. Just accept that you're in a bad mood and allow it. Acceptance is a form of serenity. Instead of fighting it, accept it and move forward.

Serenity is the ultimate goal so many of us are seeking, whether we're aware of it or not. There's a saying that *a fish doesn't know he's wet.* How would he? His entire existence is surrounded by water to the point he doesn't even knows it's there. In many ways, we're like fish living in a raging ocean of fear and stress. Our lives are spent swimming through anxiety when what we really need and crave is a sense of peace and serenity, a calm in the storm.

Make it a point to create as much serenity in your life as possible. We can't honestly expect a life without some turmoil. In fact, life might get a little boring if we didn't have *some* drama. But we also don't need to, or shouldn't have to, live a life dominated by so much angst that we don't know how unhappy we actually are until its too late.

Again, one of the best prayers to start with is *The Serenity Prayer*:

God, grant me the serenity
To accept the things I cannot change,
Courage to change the things I can,
And the wisdom to know the difference.

Repeat it as often as you need to whenever you feel you're becoming overwhelmed by fear or anxiety. Recite the words slowly, break it down and try to understand its meaning. Slowly you will feel serenity seeping into your spirit, heart and mind.

26

Ice Cream

My dad used to say to me, "Don't take everything so damn seriously! Learn how to laugh at yourself."

I think Dad realized how prone I was to overthinking everything, even as a kid. I could be so self-analyzing and self-critical that I made myself miserable. It's no wonder I needed to drink—I was driving myself insane! Who wants to go through life feeling miserable and crazy? Apparently, I did.

Whenever we get too down on ourselves, whenever we feel like the world is spinning out of control or that we've lost our way, one of the best things we can pray for is just a simple bowl of ice cream.

Maybe you don't like ice cream (*Blasphemy!*). Maybe you prefer cake or pie or cookies. The specific treat doesn't matter. What matters is that you can sometimes ask for something fun, silly and special that will uplift your spirits. Life is meant to be enjoyed. Why wallow in misery when you can wallow in ice cream?

We don't have to spend all of our free time focusing on spiritual enlightenment. Sometimes what we really need is a banana split or a hot fudge sundae to remind us how beautiful and wonderful life can be.

The point is...lighten up! Don't take yourself so damn seriously all the time.

A Prayer for Levity

Lord, today I'm just going to relax and take it easy.
Bless me with (insert your favorite ice cream here)
So that I might savor the sweetness of life.
Amen.

FOUR

Meditation

"Meditation brings wisdom; lack of
meditation leaves ignorance.
Know well what leads you forward and what holds you back,
and choose the path that leads to wisdom."
~ Buddha

"Meditation is one of the ways in which the
spiritual man keeps himself awake."
~ Thomas Merton

"Quiet the mind, and the soul will speak."
~ Ma Jaya Sati Bhagavati

27

What is Meditation?

If you mention the word "meditation" to some people, they might conjure up an image of a bedraggled hippie needing a bath and a haircut, sitting cross-legged on the floor, chanting "OM."

There are plenty of hippies practicing meditation. However, most practitioners are middle-of-the-road, everyday people like you and me, searching for a way to quiet their minds and calm their souls. Over the last fifty years, meditation has become very popular in Western culture for a good reason—it works!

Before I started meditation, I did not really understand what it was, its benefits, or how it works. You too might have similar questions.

It's generally believed that meditation as we know it today began around 1500 B.C. in India, and then developed further in China around the 6th Century B.C. Over the centuries, meditation expanded into Japan and other Eastern cultures. By the 20th Century it had reached the shores of the United States. During the 1960's counter-culture movement (those hippies), interest in meditation widened and grew. Today meditation is practiced by millions of people in the United States and around the world.

There are countless ways to describe meditation and countless books on the subject. I encourage you to read and investigate everything available on the topic. But for our purposes, I think the easiest way to describe meditation is to simply call it *mind training*.

If we can go to the gym to train our bodies, then we can go to our minds to train our thinking. Every time we practice meditation, we're trying to train our minds to be calm and quiet and to accept life as it is. In 12-step circles, this is known as *life on life's terms*.

As I mentioned early in the book, when I first tried to meditate, the noise in my brain was so loud and confusing I actually thought I might be insane. That's not an exaggeration. I seriously thought there was something wrong with me and that I might be losing touch with reality.

Every time I closed my eyes to meditate, I was confronted by multiple thoughts and ideas, all crashing together, each one demanding my attention. There was a tornado of activity swirling inside my head. But I was unable to hold a single thought for more than a few seconds before another idea or disturbing image would blow through the door of my subconscious and twist and spin across my brain.

I would quickly open my eyes, startled by the chaos inside my mind. Some thoughts were simple and amusing while others were strange and frightening. Then I would close my eyes and try again, only to quickly open them as soon as the thought-storm commenced. It was overwhelming.

Who the hell wants to do this? I asked myself. *This sucks!*

Thankfully, I stuck with it and never gave up. I hope you do the same. Over several weeks and months, I slowly began to incorporate simple techniques that allowed me to sit for longer and longer periods of time with my eyes closed while I tried my best to focus on my breath. Being able to sit with my eyes closed for five minutes was a huge accomplishment. Eventually I could sit for twenty to thirty minutes peacefully. But it took time and patience.

When I began meditation, I was searching for a way to find serenity. I knew I had a disturbed and restless ("untrained") mind. If there was a way for me to quiet the noise in my head and soothe my aching spirit, I was determined to find it. Meditation was, and is, one of the most important factors in my daily life. It has helped me immensely by calming the storms that once raged inside my head.

There are many ways to practice meditation. Like prayer, you have to find what works best for you. Most importantly, you should experiment and enjoy the journey. Meditation will help you discover how your mind operates and how to calm it. You don't have to be a hippie or a Buddhist monk either. Meditation is there for anyone and everyone who can find a few minutes in their day to pause and look inward.

28

Empty Mind

While there are many forms of meditation that have been developed by various cultures around the world, Buddhist meditation is arguably the most widely recognized and practiced. Buddhism was founded in India by Prince Siddhartha, who would later become known as The Buddha ("the awakened one" or "the enlightened one"). From India, it spread throughout the rest of the Eastern world.

It would take a lifetime to fully understand everything there is to learn and know about Buddhism. Countless books are available on the subject and I encourage you to explore its profound and beautiful teachings. Books by Thich Nhat Hahn or The Dalai Lama offer a wonderful starting point. For now, however, the easiest way to describe Buddhist meditation is the practice of *emptying the mind*.

The phrase "emptying the mind" sounds a lot like taking out the trash or cleaning out the garage. And in a way, they're very similar. When we attempt to empty our mind, we are trying to clear away the dark debris of suffering, pain, regret and angst that plague our conscious and subconscious life.

Our mind is a lot like a garage filled with junk that has accumulated over many years. We know the garage needs to be cleaned out, but we keep putting if off as long as possible. Then one day we turn on the light and are confronted by a mountain of rubbish. Sooner or later, we have to empty the garage or the problem is going to keep getting worse.

When I first confronted the rubbish heap in my own brain, I was shocked by how much garbage I had been hoarding. It's amazing to look back on it now and realize the amount of negative data I had accumulated over my lifetime. My mind was filled with anger, resentment and fear. It was very difficult and sometimes painful to look inside and explore my own thoughts.

As I advanced in my meditation practice, I began to learn that most of my negative thoughts were a result of selfish craving. I craved wealth, power, popularity, sex, influence and glory. I wanted the world to recognize my greatness and adore me. But since that wasn't how things had turned out, my cravings had turned into bitterness.

One of the great things about meditation, particularly Buddhist meditation, is that it allows us an opportunity to first recognize our source of suffering in order to release it. If we're able to see what is causing us pain (negative thought), we can then identify it for what it is and let it go with a smile. We have the ability to train our minds in order to release the negative thoughts that hold us hostage. Empty our minds of destructive cravings and our minds will fill with peace and acceptance.

I often use the image of a red helium balloon being released into the sky. Once I have identified a negative thought, instead of holding onto it, I think of it as a balloon that I want to float away. I let it go and watch as it drifts upwards into the clouds, finally disappearing out of sight. Perhaps it sounds too simplistic, but it often works.

There are times when negative thoughts are buried so deep, and are so painful, that we need to seek professional help to dislodge them. But meditation can be helpful to almost anyone looking to explore the inner workings of their mind so that they can begin letting go of the harmful debris they've been hoarding.

29

Soul Food

As important as it is to empty our minds of negative thoughts, it's equally important to fill our souls with love, compassion and optimism.

Judeo-Christian meditation places an emphasis on inviting God into one's mind, body and soul by focusing on specific biblical passages or ideas. We can take a sentence, paragraph or chapter from the Bible and contemplate its words and meaning. Buddhist meditation also offers numerous chants, mantras, poems and prayers that can be explored and contemplated during meditation.

The point is to feed our souls with nourishing words that provide uplifting and transcendent thoughts and ideas.

If you were to take a glass filled with dirty, brown pond water and hold it under a dripping faucet, eventually the drops of water from the sink would replace the dirty pond water. The glass would then be filled with water clean enough to drink and nourish your body.

This is similar to how contemplative meditation works. We add a steady drip of daily transcendent wisdom into our minds by contemplating a passage, poem, prayer or mantra that feeds and nourishes our souls.

Emile Coue was a French psychologist who developed a method of psychotherapy based on optimistic autosuggestion. He created the following mantra: *"Every day, in every way, I'm getting better and better."*

Coue taught that by repeating this simple mantra over and over during meditation, preferably daily or even hourly, we will experience a new reality. Our life will begin to improve because we are feeding our souls an uplifting message of hope.

There are many ways that you can feed your soul and nourish your mind. Those might include a passage from the Bible, a Buddhist chant or a beautiful poem. But it's important that you become aware of what you're consuming. What you feed your mind and soul is just as important as what you feed your body.

Are you drinking a glass filled with dirty pond water or clean, filtered water? Are you living on a steady diet of negativity and pessimism or positivity and hope?

30

Active Meditation

One of the great things about meditation is that there are so many different styles and ways to practice. As they saying goes, variety is the spice of life. You don't have to just sit in the lotus position with legs crossed and eyes closed. There are many ways to meditate that will keep it varied and interesting.

I tend to have a short attention span. I'm also very restless and have a difficult time sitting in one place for an extended period of time. What I've discovered is that meditation doesn't necessarily require sitting in one spot all the time. Active meditation, for me, has been one of the best ways to clear my mind.

Certain activities lend themselves quite well to meditation. Yoga, walking, jogging and swimming are all good ways to empty the mind. The idea is to engage in a repetitive activity that allows you an opportunity to focus on one thing—your breath. Following your breath is one of the simplest and readily available methods of meditation. I'll go into more detail about following your breath in a later chapter, but for now just think of your breath as a focal point to guide you, like a point of light in the darkness.

I started fishing when I was a young boy. My father taught my brothers and me how to fish and I've pursued it on and off for most of my life. Today I'm an avid fly fisherman and spend as much of my free time as possible on the Truckee River, fishing for rainbow trout. For me, fishing has become much more than just a sport and a pastime; it's my passion.

Fly fishing requires rhythm and focus. You're in constant motion, trying to cast your line into specific areas of the water, and then concentrating on the line as it drifts downriver. During the drift, you have to watch your line for any subtle movement or hesitation. Then you set the hook quickly if you feel a fish grab your fly below the surface.

When I'm fishing, I try to follow my breath while casting and during the drift. There are times that I become so engaged in the rhythm of *cast-breath-drift, cast-breath-drift, cast-breath-drift,* I completely forget where I am or how much time has passed. I can be on the river for hours at a time and barely notice.

Of course, when I do hook into a fish, my concentration is broken by a rush of adrenaline. But once I catch the fish (and release it back into the water) and the excitement recedes, I easily slip back into my quiet *cast-breath-drift* rhythm. After a full day of fishing, I'm usually completely relaxed and sleep like a baby that night.

Meditation doesn't have to become stale and boring. There are many activities that will assist you in your practice. If you enjoy yoga, then try following your breath during each pose. Try different things. Even walking your dog can be a perfect opportunity to meditate. The idea is to find a good rhythm, and focus on your breath as if it's a beam of light.

31

Simplicity

Before I began exploring meditation on my own, I had the impression that it involved a highly esoteric, complicated set of rules and rituals. In my mind, the only people who knew how to meditate were Hindu monastics and Buddhist monks. I envisioned a secret society of bald guys in orange robes, chanting in unison in a room thick with incense smoke and candles. The idea of breaking this secret code seemed impossible.

So, I put it off as long as I could, too lazy and scared to learn the truth. Eventually, though, I realized that I had to do something about my anxiety and depression. I had been struggling with fear, angst and depression since I was around fourteen years old. There were days when my mood was so dark that I couldn't get out of bed or leave the house. I had used alcohol to self-medicate but drinking was no longer an option. So, I needed to find a way to soothe my aching mind.

Before I tried meditation, I began to read about it. I seriously had no idea what it was or how to start, so I read books on the topic. What I quickly learned is that meditation doesn't need to be complicated. In fact, the simpler I keep it, the better. My image of bald monks in smoky temples didn't match the reality.

Meditation, like prayer, is an individual journey that can be, and should be, tailored to each person. You have to find what works best for you. And not every day is going to be the same. One day you might want to sit inside on a chair or on the floor and meditate. Another day you may prefer to sit outside on the porch, in a park, or on the beach. You might prefer to meditate during yoga another day. What's important is that you find a simple way to focus your mind and not complicate the process.

In the next section, I will go into more detail and provide a number of easy suggestions that you can try. But for now, the simplest way to meditate is to sit comfortably in a chair or on a couch with legs crossed or not, close your eyes and *focus on your breath.*

Breathe naturally through your nostrils. You don't need to pant or exaggerate each breath, just follow the normal flow of air as it passes in and out of your nose. Feel your chest and shoulders gently rise and fall with each breath. As thoughts come into your mind, push them aside. Then bring your attention back to your breath. Focus only on your breath. It's as simple as that.

Meditation doesn't need to be complicated. If you're completely new to it, you can try it for just two or three minutes. Then you can try it twice per day. As you get used to it, increase the amount of time you meditate to five minutes. Eventually you'll find it easier and easier to sit for longer stretches of time without even noticing.

Keep it simple and enjoy the ride.

32

Benefits

Since I began meditating, there have been brief periods when I stopped for various reasons. Usually it's just from excessive laziness. Or, perhaps when I'm fighting a bad cold or the flu and can't muster the energy to roll out of bed. But I definitely notice a change in my attitude and outlook on life when there's a pause in my meditation practice.

I've noticed that any time I go more than a few days without meditation, my mood changes. I start to become irritable, easily frustrated and just plain cranky. I grow more temperamental, sleep less, and feel less calm and optimistic. How I survived so long without it is a mystery.

I learned long ago that my emotional life is like a boat floating on an unpredictable ocean of competing currents and sudden storms. One day it's blue skies and calm water, the next day its pounding rain and raging waves. Meditation is the ballast that keeps my boat from capsizing.

One of the great gifts of meditation is the ability to turn our focus away from our daily strife and struggle so that we can concentrate on stillness. This doesn't mean we ignore or discard what's going on in our life. All the meditation in the world won't change the fact that we have to work, pay bills and be responsible adults. But meditation allows you a period of respite from the turmoil and enables you to calm your mind, body and soul. In other words, it keeps your boat afloat.

Many of the benefits associated with meditation are mental and emotional. But numerous studies have proven that there are many physical benefits to meditation as well. Meditation has been proven to:

- Calm the mind
- Reduce stress
- Improve emotional well-being
- Increase focus and attention
- Enhance self-awareness
- Increase optimism and hope
- Reduce panic attacks
- Improve sleep
- Lower blood pressure
- Reduce anxiety and depression

This is just a partial list of benefits. The more you practice, the more results you'll receive. Meditation is without a doubt one of the best things you will ever do for yourself. And like prayer, it doesn't cost anything.

We have the best medicine and therapy available to us right where we sit. If you're anything like me, once you start meditation, you'll wonder how you survived so long without it.

FIVE

Meditation with Focus

"Where there is peace and meditation,
there is neither anxiety nor doubt."
~ *Sr. Francis de Sales*

"Meditation is not a way of making your mind quiet.
It's a way of entering into the quiet that's already there,
buried under the 50,000 thoughts the
average person thinks every day."
~ *Deepak Chopra*

33

Posture

My father demanded that my brothers and I sit properly at the dinner table. We were expected to sit straight in our chair, napkin in our lap, and use our fork and knife properly. No eating with our fingers. And no slouching was allowed. Most importantly, we could never, *ever* put our elbows on the table until dinner was finished. Putting our elbows on the table was absolutely forbidden, like a mortal sin.

Of course, being kids, we had to question everything. We battled with him over these rules throughout our childhood. And as we got older, we had many debates over the subject of proper table manners. My older brothers, Scott and Rhett, were particularly fond of questioning these seemingly arbitrary and archaic rules.

"Who cares how we sit?" they demanded. "What difference does it make?"

My dad, always patient with his rebellious brood of boys, would just smile.

"Bad posture shows a negative attitude," Dad would inform us. "Good posture shows a positive attitude."

The same is true in seated meditation. The physical attention we give to meditation—our body's posture—reflects, and affects, our attitude and state of mind. It is important to sit in a strong, upright position in order to establish a positive intention and focus.

- If you choose to sit during your meditation instead of engaging in an activity like walking or yoga, sit in an upright position with a straight spine. Don't slouch. A straight, upright position will help your mind stay alert and will open your chest for easier breathing.

- You can sit in a comfortable chair, on a floor cushion, or on a couch or a bed.

- If you're flexible enough, you can try a lotus position (both feet over both knees) or half lotus position (one foot over one knee). Because I have an old sports injury in one of my knees, I prefer to use a simple cross-legged posture like kids often use (both ankles under my legs).

- If you choose to sit in a chair, sit in a normal upright position with both feet on the floor.

- Rest your hands comfortably on your knees, palms up. Or, you can cup your hands together and rest them just below your navel with your thumb tips touching.

- Softly close your eyes.
- Take several deep breaths, filling your lungs with air. Then exhale through your mouth.
- Once you have taken several deep breaths, slow your breathing and let the air flow in and out of your nose. Slow your breath until you're breathing naturally.
- Don't force your breath. Just let it flow in and out, slowly and quietly.
- Feel your chest and shoulders softly rise and fall with each breath.
- If your mind begins to wander and thoughts crowd your brain, don't get frustrated or angry. Just bring your attention back to your breath. This is going to happen a lot at first; your mind will wander. You will be bombarded by thoughts and images. That's okay. Just let it happen and keep coming back to your breath.

In the beginning, don't worry about how much time you spend meditating. I used to obsess over how many minutes I could sit with my eyes closed, focusing on my breath. It felt like a self-imposed competition. In fact, I thought about it so much that it became a distraction. Just do the best you can. Whether it's two minutes or twenty, you're doing something positive for yourself. So, don't obsess over the minutes. Instead, focus on your posture and your breath and forget about time.

34

Chattering Monkeys

The Buddha used the term "Monkey Mind" to describe how our minds jump from thought to thought, just like a monkey in a tree, jumping from branch to branch. Every time the monkey grasps one branch, it immediately reaches for another branch, swinging from one to another in perpetual motion, never resting in the present moment.

Scientists estimate that we have from 50,000 to 70,000 thoughts per day. We're constantly swinging from one thought to another, rarely taking a break. It's exhausting!

I refer to the constant motion and noise in my brain as chattering monkeys. Not only are the monkeys swinging from one branch to another, they're also screeching and chattering in a non-stop attempt for attention. *Look at me! Look at me! Look at me!*

As I described earlier, when I first confronted the chattering monkeys in my brain, I was overwhelmed and a little frightened. I would close my eyes and try to meditate only to be bombarded by ceaseless and wild thoughts and images, all screaming for attention.

I wondered, *Is this normal? Am I insane? What the hell is wrong with me?*

At first it seemed impossible to calm my mind and turn down the volume on the constant chatter. I would close my eyes and become so shocked by the cacophony of noise in my head that I'd immediately open my eyes like a child frightened by the dark. *Quick, turn on the light!*

I believe that one of the main reasons I drank alcoholically for so long was to shut down and silence all the noise in my head.

One very important thing I've learned from meditation is *acceptance*.

If we can first *accept*, without judgment or fear, that we have very active minds, then we can begin to calm and quiet our minds through the discipline of meditation.

Does this mean the chattering monkeys will ever go away completely? Sorry, no. We're human beings and humans have very powerful, active brains, which have created amazing and wonderful things during our time on earth. But we can, through meditation, quiet the chaos for brief periods in order to enjoy stillness, serenity and peace. A brief calm in the storm is sometimes just what we need to rejuvenate our mind and soul if we want to face the challenges of life with fresh energy.

So, when you close your eyes and the monkeys start to swing from branch to branch, screaming for your attention, just accept them as welcome friends who need to take a brief rest while you enjoy the peace.

35

Passing Clouds

When I was a young boy, I loved to lie in the grass, watching billowy white clouds passing across the blue sky. I looked for shapes in the clouds—boats, faces and animals. It was a peaceful and fun way to pass the time and stimulate my imagination. How wonderful it would have been if I were able to reach up and touch the clouds as they passed, moving and shaping them as I pleased.

In many ways, the activities of your mind are like passing clouds that we can move and shape to some degree.

"Chattering monkeys" is an appropriate metaphor for the often aggressive and even hostile thoughts that we encounter when we're just learning how to meditate. But "passing clouds" can be a more accurate and friendly way to view our thoughts after our meditation has evolved.

Once you've learned to accept that you have a very active and noisy mind (monkeys), it eventually becomes easier to see your thoughts not as chattering beasts but rather as harmless clouds passing across your mind's eye. Each cloud has its own shape and size. Some are dark and seem menacing, while others are white and puffy, like harmless cotton.

But that's all they are—passing clouds. You can either let them linger and frighten you or, even better, you can simply let them pass and continue on their journey across the sky. Think of your passing thoughts as harmless passing clouds drifting across your mind from one ear to another, passing out of sight as you lie back and enjoy the view.

36

Smile

There are times when the clothes we wear affect how we feel. When we walk into a room wearing our favorite shirt or blouse, we'll automatically express confidence without even trying. There is just something about wearing certain clothes that makes us feel good about ourselves and the image we project to the world.

Wearing a smile can also boost our confidence and change how we feel, even when we meditate. This is a trick I learned years ago and I use it often, especially when I'm in a bad mood.

When you start to meditate, simply close your eyes and smile. You don't have to smile big and wide with your teeth exposed. If you do that, you'll just feel weird. Instead, turn the corners of your mouth up slightly in a soft smile. Entering your meditation this way can have a huge impact on how you feel.

If you start your meditation in a dark, angry mood (frowning), you will often remain that way during the entire experience. But if you enter with a smile, your mood will quickly become more positive.

I find that this holds true outside of meditation as well. Some days I just feel like crap. I wake up in a bad mood, or I'm facing some difficulties that make me anxious or depressed. Instead of giving into these dark moods, if I can smile, it sometimes has a huge impact on my attitude and outlook.

Scientific studies show that smiling releases dopamine, endorphins and serotonin into our brains. These are our feel-good neurotransmitters (also known as "happy chemicals"). These transmitters have an immediate impact on one's mood and state of well-being. At the same time, smiling decreases stress hormones and lowers blood pressure. Smiling also sends a signal to the world that we're not a threat. It can relieve tension for ourselves and those we encounter.

I'm not suggesting that you walk around with a huge grin all the time, like a lunatic. You don't want to frighten people. But a well-timed smile throughout the day can go a long way to altering your mood. And a slight smile during meditation can have an enormous impact on how quickly you can calm your mind and find peace.

37

What Is This?

Mantras are words, phrases or sounds that are repeated over and over to boost concentration during meditation. Mantras are often spoken or chanted aloud in order to illicit their rhythmic and vibrational powers to soothe the spirit and focus the mind. They can be extremely effective. I highly recommend trying a mantra yourself, especially if you have a mind that wanders easily or you find it difficult to concentrate for more than a few minutes.

I go through periods when I simply can't get my mind to quiet down. Even though I've been practicing meditation for years, I still struggle with a very noisy brain. There are times that it won't settle down, no matter what. When this happens, I resort to my favorite mantra.

"What Is This?" is a silent mantra that has worked for me without fail over the years. While there are plenty of more esoteric or cool-sounding mantras you can choose from (like "Nam Myoho Renge Kyo,"), the

one I always rely on is *What Is This?* It has consistently worked for me.

Repeating this mantra silently with my eyes closed is always an amazing, interesting experience. It starts out as a simple question about my meditation. As I continue to repeat the mantra, it begins to take on different meaning. The question seems to shift and change color, taking me deeper and deeper into relaxation. I don't attempt to answer the questions. I just ask the question over and over, slowly, gently.

In addition to asking the question, *What Is This?* I also move the emphasis from one word to another.

What Is *This?*

What Is This?

What *Is* This?

I allow the words to float in front of my mind's eye, passing like clouds, as I repeat the question in different ways.

Just to be clear, there is no answer to the question—or not that I know of, anyway. It's the question itself that matters. By repeating it over and over, slowly, silently, for ten or fifteen minutes, my find always starts to calm down. The words become comforting and familiar, quieting the noise in my brain.

Give it a try if you're struggling with the cacophony in your own head. And if you ever do find the answer to the question *What Is This?* please let me know.

38

The idea of sitting cross-legged on the ground, chanting "OM" has become a bit of a cliché. It's the stereotypical image, almost a cartoon image, many people have of meditation. But chanting is one of the most effective and relaxing methods to clear your mind. It's not an accident that it's been used for centuries by millions of people. It works and should be included in your grab bag of meditation tools.

There are many sounds, words and mantras that can be used in meditation. As I mentioned earlier, there are plenty of esoteric, cool-sounding mantras and chants like "Nam Myoho Renge Kyo" that have amazing power and are wonderful to experiment with during meditation. But the easiest one to start with is good old-fashioned "OM." It's simple, clear, effective and can be used by anyone.

One of the most powerful sounds in the universe is that of a mother humming to her baby. She holds her child close to her breast, humming and rocking quietly. The child can hear and *feel* the soothing vibration emanating from her chest. The vibration immediately calms and comforts the child.

Chanting "OM" is similar to a mother's hum, except that it comes from within your own chest. "OM" is said to have the same vibrational frequency as everything in the universe. If that's true, then chanting "OM" connects you to the entire universe through sound. Therefore, when you use "OM" to meditate, you become one with universe. In fact, your body *becomes* the universe. How cool is that?!

"OM" is pronounced with three sounds: A, U, M. So as you chant the word, draw it out so it sounds like "**AOOOOMMM**..." followed by a few seconds of silence.

Try this:

- Sit in a comfortable position with a straight spine. (Remember, good posture.)
- Close your eyes
- Take a few deep breaths
- Begin to chant slowly and quietly "AOOOMMM"
- Let the word trail off into silence for a few seconds and then repeat
- As you repeat the word, let it flow out from your chest
- Notice the vibration as it flows throughout your body

- Focus on the word and the vibration as you continue to repeat it
- Try chanting for 5—10 minutes to start

39

Music and Sound

For many people, meditating to music or ambient sound is one of the best ways they can get themselves to relax and concentrate.

When I first began to experiment with different methods of meditation, I purchased several meditation CD's consisting of soft, ambient sounds and music. (Today you can download them directly to your smart phone.)

I found this method to be extremely helpful, especially in the early days of my practice when my ability to concentrate was limited. If I wanted to meditate for longer periods, thirty minutes or longer, I simply wasn't able to sit for that long on my own. Meditation music and sounds helped me meditate for long periods of time and always left me feeling calm and refreshed.

In addition to music, there are soundtracks available for meditation, capturing nature sounds, such as waves, rainfall, streams, rivers, and chirping crickets. These sounds can be incredibly soothing and can help calm your mind while you focus on your breath.

Another benefit I discovered with many of these sounds was this: if I put them on next to my bed, my sleep was often much deeper and more relaxing than usual. In my early days of recovery, good sleep was difficult to achieve. I found that many of these ambient sounds and meditation music helped me sleep soundly through the night.

Experimenting with various sounds and music might be the perfect way for *you* to begin or deepen your meditation practice.

40

Yoga

I f you've never attempted yoga, it's time to start. Yes, I know it looks difficult, awkward and sort of goofy. But yoga is one of the best things you can do for your body and mind. I highly recommend it. There are yoga classes for beginners in every community in the United States. Start with a simple "gentle yoga" class and you will be amazed how good it feels.

During the early days of my sobriety, I was in bad physical shape. I was overweight, had high blood pressure, and could barely walk up a flight of stairs without wheezing. I slowly started to improve my health by taking long walks every day. Eventually, I joined a local gym and started jogging on the treadmill and lifting weights.

A friend suggested that I add yoga into my workout routine. This seemed ridiculous to me at first. To my way of thinking at the time, taking a yoga class was the same as taking a ballet class. My reaction was, "No thanks. I'll pass!"

But my friend persisted. So, eventually I gave in and joined a beginners' class at my gym. I have to admit, my first few attempts at yoga were pretty pathetic. My body was stiffer than a frozen pretzel. I could barely stretch. But I discovered that after each class, even when it was difficult, my entire body felt relaxed. And yoga seemed to supply me with energy and a more positive mood.

I quickly became a yoga addict. Finally, an addiction that was actually good for me!

One of the best aspects of yoga is the fact that it lends itself so well to meditation. In fact, yoga is *its own* form of meditation. Once you've learned the basics and get past any feelings of awkwardness, the flow of yoga is a great way to practice mindfulness.

If you can focus all your attention on each movement and pose, as well as your breath, then your mind will quiet down and discard all other thought. You will become completely immersed in the yoga. Much like chanting, the exercise itself becomes your thought and you will experience a respite from all negative mind activity.

Yoga is also a great form of exercise and will improve your physical fitness. Combined with its intrinsic meditative qualities, yoga is a smart choice for just about everyone.

41

Loving-Kindness

s unconditional love possible? Is it a real thing or just a myth?

It's easy to point to a mother's devotion to her child as proof that unconditional love exists in the world. But beyond this one example, can we love others without judgement, no matter what? Even people we don't know or people who have hurt us? Is it possible to cultivate compassion and empathy for *everyone*?

Loving-kindness is unconditional love for everyone and everything. Loving-kindness is the greatest hope we have of surviving peacefully on earth.

It's not an easy goal to achieve, finding something to love in every person. Trust me, I struggle with it myself all the time. People hurt each other every day. People can be rude, petty and spiteful. Human beings can be unpredictable and cruel, capable of horrible acts of violence. Animals, too. Don't believe me? Try kissing a wild grizzly bear on the nose.

Human history is filled with war, genocide, fear and hate. It's a wonder we survived the 20th Century without blowing up the planet. Apparently, God's patience with us is limitless. But what we often choose to ignore, and doesn't get much coverage in our newspapers, is the fact that human history is also filled with countless stories of kindness, and selfless acts of heroism, charity and deep love.

One of the best examples of the contrast between love and hate in the human race is the terrorist attacks that occurred on September 11th, 2001 when nineteen religious fanatics blinded by hatred murdered nearly 3,000 people they didn't know. The viciousness and cruelty are unfathomable.

On that same day, however, thousands of firefighters, police officers, and other first responders walked headlong into the inferno in order to help their fellow citizens. And countless people helped one another in the hours, days and months that followed this pointless attack. Ultimately, human love surpassed human hate, as it always does.

Hatred does exist in the human heart. There is no doubt. And we are all capable of tapping into it if we're not careful. But love, the greatest force in the universe, is also a very distinct and deeply-rooted aspect of our humanity.

To cultivate love, compassion and forgiveness, even for those who wish to harm us, is the single most important thing we can strive for in our lifetime on earth.

We must find a way to forgive others (and ourselves) of any misdeeds, and attempt to always find the best in everyone. And we must understand that many people are so blinded by fear, ignorance and sadness that they lash out at others with cruelty and often violence.

If we encounter a stray dog, do we hate the dog if it bites us? Or do we understand that the dog is probably reacting out of fear and ignorance of our intention? The dog is only doing what he thinks he must do to survive. There is no point in hating or resenting the dog. Instead, we should cultivate compassion and understanding for it—and then go to the doctor for a rabies shot.

I'm not suggesting that people who hurt others shouldn't be punished. In many cases, they should—but we must rely on the rule of law, especially when violence or murder is involved. But it's crucial to start practicing loving-kindness towards everyone and everything. Otherwise, we will suffocate on our own resentment, fear and hatred, just like those who have harmed us.

Try this during your meditation:

- Sit in a comfortable position
- Close your eyes and breathe deeply
- Slow your breath then silently repeat these words:

May I be free from resentment.
May I be free from anger.
May I be joyous and kind.
May I always forgive.

THE SOBER JOURNEY

May I love all beings.
May I bring kindness into the world.

Repeat these words throughout your meditation, in any order you wish. Let them float in front of you. Savor their meaning and let them settle deep into your heart.

42

This Too Shall Pass

earning to live in acceptance is the key to living a life of peace and serenity.

When we use the term "acceptance," we're not talking about resignation, which implies giving up or allowing bad things to happen. We're not doormats to be stepped on. Acceptance as we want to use the word means *non-resistance*. We want to be able to reach a point where we can *accept* things that happen in our life (and in our mind) and observe them without fear or judgment.

To use a well-worn sports analogy, life throws us a lot of curve balls. It often seems that our problems appear out of nowhere. We start the day with a certain set of expectations, only to be thrown a curve ball that catches us off guard, sometimes hitting us square in the face. If we become too fixated on, or attached to, how things *should be* instead of accepting how of things *actually are*, we become trapped in a never-ending cycle of disappointment and frustration.

Some days we're hit by more than one curve ball at a time. Then we find ourselves trying to fix one problem while confronting another. We become overwhelmed and can easily succumb to frustration and anger. At this point, we might want to just throw our hands up in the air and resign ourselves to our miserable fate.

But there's another path we can take: acceptance.

One of the greatest phrases I've used over the years is, "*This too shall pass.*"

The fact is, *all* things shall pass eventually. Nothing is permanent. Bad, unpleasant or frightening things all end at some point. The same is true for good things. *All things shall pass.* The trick is to accept conditions as impermanent rather than obsessing over or attaching ourselves to anything—good or bad.

One moment might seem perfect; the next moment might be filled with problems. One day you might be dating your soul mate; the next day your heart is broken. One week you might feel healthy; the next week you're sick. One month you might have money in the bank; the next month you're broke.

All of these are passing conditions. Nothing is permanent and nothing stays the same. The only thing we can rely on is change itself. Change is the only constant. Both the bad and the good will all pass into something else at some point. If we can accept this fact, if we can live in *acceptance of what is, rather than what should be,* we will find it much easier to live in harmony with the fluctuations and changes that confront us every day.

Again, we don't want to be doormats and let life (or people) trample over us. We have to take responsibility and fix things that need to be fixed. But it's also important to realize that life is filled with ups and downs and there is no such thing as perfection.

Life just is. Therefore, when you're being bombarded by curve balls, simply remind yourself of this truth: "*This too shall pass.*"

The same is true in meditation. You will sometimes have thoughts that are disturbing or upsetting. Sometimes you will be overwhelmed by too many thoughts, all demanding your attention at the same time. Instead of fighting and resisting, just accept without judgment or fear. Focus on your breathing and repeat the phrase: "*This too shall pass.*

43

Start Today

The only way to learn something new is to start. You can read everything in the world on any subject, but until you start, you'll never reap the benefits of whatever it is you're trying to learn. You can't learn a new language, for example, just by reading about it. You have to start speaking it too.

Prayer and meditation are both wonderful topics to read about and discuss. Both are subjects I've spent years reading about myself. But if you want to enjoy the experience and reap the rewards of either or both, you need to start practicing them today. Not tomorrow. Not next week. Today!

Many people feel that meditation in particular is too esoteric and foreign for them to understand and enjoy. But it's really quite simple; *sit down, close your eyes, focus on your breath*. Over time you can begin to explore other forms of meditation and go deeper in your practice. But if you haven't started yet, then start with the basics.

Procrastination has always been one of my worst character defects. I'm lazy by nature and will do anything I can to put off today whatever I can do tomorrow (or next month). I've always been that way. Even as a kid, I would put off doing chores or homework as long as possible. As an adult, I've always hated doing laundry. I will let the dirty clothes pile up until I have nothing left to wear. Only then will I do a load of laundry. It's just how I'm wired.

The same was true with meditation. I put if off for years while I pursued more immediate gratification from a bottle. I chose to numb my mind rather than awaken it.

I truly believe that if I had started practicing prayer and meditation at an earlier age, I would have avoided much of the pain and harm I inflicted on myself over many years of hard drinking. Prayer and meditation have provided me with the only long-term comfort and serenity I have ever been able to find within myself.

Am I at peace one hundred percent of the time? No, absolutely not. I'm human. I have good days and bad days. I can be moody, lazy and temperamental. But I always try my best to be the best that I can be. And my best begins with prayer and meditation. At this point in my life, I rarely go a day without either. Prayer and meditation are the nutrients that feed my soul. And most days, they keep me sane.

So, if you haven't started yet, start today. Who knows, maybe you too will find the peace you've been seeking.

SIX

The Big G Word

"Faith is taking the first step even when
you can't see the whole staircase."
~ *Rev. Martin Luther King Jr.*

"i thank You God for most this amazing
day: for the leaping greenly spirits of trees
and a blue true dream of sky; and for everything
which is natural which is infinite which is yes"
~ *E.E. Cummings*

"Be still and know that I am God."
~ *Psalm 46:10*

44

Who is God?

So many people seem to have an aversion to the word "God" these days. We're living through a strange time of political correctness, where certain words offend a few people (I call them the *Thought Police*) to such a degree that the rest of the population lives in constant fear of expressing themselves.

For some reason, the Thought Police have determined that using the word God has become tantamount to coercion or assault. To openly express faith in God has somehow become a form of repression or attack on non-believers. For those who do have faith in a Higher Power, it often feels safer to just keep it to themselves and not express their beliefs at all. Otherwise, we risk retribution or ridicule, or both.

It often feels like faith has been replaced by cynicism. Many people seem to believe in politicians more than they do in God.

Call it what you wish—*God, The Great Spirit, The Tao, The One, The Creator, The Supreme Being, The Force* (for you *Star Wars* fans)—but having faith in a power greater than ourselves is, and always has been, an intrinsic part of being human.

Ever since mankind appeared on earth, humans have felt that there was something beyond what can be seen or heard. There has always been a deep curiosity about that which is beyond our sight, a powerful feeling that there is something or someone else with us whose presence can be sensed but not quite grasped or completely understood.

Ancient cultures often assigned this innate feeling to multiple Gods like Zeus, Poseidon and Apollo. Native American faith has focused on a broader spiritual presence (*The Great Spirit*), as have certain segments of Chinese culture (*The Tao*). Judaism, Islam and Christianity all hold monotheistic faith in a single God who oversees all creation and is involved in, and concerned with, mankind's activity on earth.

Christians in particular believe that God's presence was made manifest on earth through Jesus Christ. God was so concerned with mankind that he entered time and space for a brief period in order to instruct us as to how we should treat one another through love. But the Thought Police of his time didn't like what Jesus had to say, so they took it upon themselves to have him executed. Political correctness 2000 years ago could be very violent—a warning for all of us today.

As I stated earlier, I believe that *all spiritual roads lead to God, but not all of us are driving in the same car to get there.*

The question, "*Who Is God?*" has to be discovered by each of us on our own. We can seek instruction from others, and plant our faith in the doctrine that best fits our need. But ultimately, we have to seek out the answer through our own heart and mind.

Most importantly, you should never be afraid to express your belief in *God, The Tao, The Great Spirit or your Higher Power*. Shout it from the rooftops, if you want to, regardless of what the Thought Police try to demand of you.

45

One Source

I believe that all religions point to the same thing: a conscious source of logic and love in the universe. There are numerous names given to this Higher Power: *Jehovah, Yahweh, Allah, Jesus, Jah, Vishnu,* to name just a few. But all the major religions, no matter what name they use, share the view that all existence, including humanity, developed from a single source or cause.

God—the one source—is the *cause,* while life is the *effect* or manifestation.

Let's take this concept a step further. Since all life comes from the same source, then all life is one life. If God gave birth to one, she gave life to all. All life, then, comes from the same parent source.

So, it really doesn't matter, in my opinion, what you call the One Source of all life. Call it Fred or Janet if you want. Call it Mr. Doorknob. It really makes no difference. What matters is your willingness to have faith that the source of all life is a source of love, given freely and in infinite abundance. The very essence of life, the most powerful force in the universe, is love. God is love and love is God.

"Agape" is a Greek term meaning *"love that comes from God"* or *"the love of God for man, and of man for God."* It's a term that captures the basic essence of what the role of God can and should be in our lives. Agape love is pure and unconditional, like the love of a mother for her child.

So why wouldn't we want to put our trust and faith in a love so divine? For me, it was all about *ego*.

For many years I fed on my own ego like a starving man feasting on a giant Thanksgiving turkey, persisting even after I was left with only an empty turkey carcass. I tried to do it all on my own, blindly putting all my faith in my own ability to control the world and the universe. I was the master of my own destiny.

Who needed God? Not me. And look how that turned out! I ended up a frightened, sick alcoholic, crying out for help, face down on a filthy motel floor.

The moment I gave up trying to run the universe and handed my life over to a power greater than myself, everything changed. I took myself out of the driver's seat and became a passenger.

I didn't worry about what to call my Higher Power. I didn't have to assign a name to it. I joyfully gave up fighting and gave in to faith in something beyond me, finally recognizing that the One Source of all life was *for* me, not *against* me.

46

Faith, Not Guilt

think that a lot of people are turned off by all the guilt that often seems to be associated with organized religion. Shame and guilt have been used by many religious leaders over the centuries to coerce people into adhering to predetermined rules and rituals. Those who balk often face the threat of expulsion from the religion or eternal damnation to hell. Upon close inspection, many of these rules feel arbitrary and meaningless, especially to people who are exploring faith for the first time as adults.

Granted, we live in a time in history when "morality" is a fluid term. What we consider moral one day might be deemed antiquated and trivial the next day. It's difficult to keep up with the ever-shifting definition of right and wrong when the rules are always changing.

Organized religion is an area of society that has, traditionally, solidified a set of rules to follow. But when we don't follow those rules exactly as expressed by the religious doctrine, we are often saddled with guilt and shame.

Guilt and shame can be powerful and often destructive forces that turn many people off of religion. But faith itself doesn't necessarily require adherence to one religion or another. For some people, faith in God or a Higher Power is an individual journey of discovery and exploration, rather than a forced set of standards and rules. Ultimately, we each have to find our own pathway to God.

Personally, I feel just as comfortable in a Catholic church as I do in a Buddhist temple. And quite often, I find it just as easy to commune with God while sitting next to a river or lake as I do in a church or temple.

As I want to always emphasize, I think religion plays a very important role in society, and I encourage you to find and explore whatever religion best suits your needs and circumstances. But faith should not, in my opinion, be wrapped up in guilt and shame. Faith should be associated with peace and joy. It should bring us calm and understanding—never sadness or guilt.

Whatever path you choose to follow to develop a conscious contact with God, may it always be a journey of love rather than shame.

47

Religion

When we pray, we don't necessarily have to restrict ourselves to a pre-set system of rules, beliefs and traditions in order to connect, or commune, with God. Religion is irrelevant to prayer. You don't have to belong to any particular religion in order to commune with God or Spirit.

If we choose to put our faith in a higher conscious force, a Universal Holy Spirit, then our faith journey begins within our own body and mind. We have the ability to bridge the gap between the secular and the sacred through our own spiritual energy. We can love God, and connect with God, by simply speaking with God in our own way.

Perhaps you feel cynical towards organized religion. Many people find it difficult to accept that God is available through only one singular system of beliefs. But what if *every* religion is the "correct" religion? What if *all* the religions of the world are actually saying the same thing, just using different languages, symbols and rituals to convey the same message?

Every major organized religion shares a similar goal: to bring humanity closer to God. Religion, at its core, is simply a bridge between the secular and the sacred, between the human spirit and the Supreme Spirit.

Maybe you have some type of trauma connected to religion. Or, if you're like me, you had *no* religious training as a child and might simply be uninformed about what organized religion is and the purpose it serves.

Ultimately, your view of religion does not really matter. What matters is your willingness to pray and communicate with an ultimate power beyond yourself. You don't need a specific system of beliefs or a rigid doctrine in order to connect with God. You only need a willingness to try.

48

The Unseen

ife is filled with things we cannot see or touch and yet we have complete faith in their existence. Electricity and gravity are two obvious examples I used earlier.

Electricity is a form of energy that results from the existence of charged particles like electrons or protons. It allows us to turn on the lights in our home and run our computers. Gravity is a force by which our planet draws objects towards its center. Gravity keeps us attached to the earth. Both electricity and gravity are real. Of course, we can't *see* either of them but we do experience their impact on our lives every day. Each time we turn on a light, we experience electricity. Every time we jump into the air and land safely back on our feet, we experience gravity.

Love and air are similar to electricity and gravity. We can't actually see or touch either, but we get to experience the effects of each. Air fills our lungs so that we can breathe. Love fills our souls and gives our lives meaning. Without any of these phenomena, our species couldn't survive on earth.

So it is, I believe, with God. Just because we can't see or physically touch God doesn't mean that God isn't there, any more than we could deny the existence of electricity, gravity, air or love.

All of these things existed before man appeared on earth. Discovering them has taken us thousands of years. Electricity existed when humans were living in caves, and the same is true of gravity and air. We just hadn't discovered them yet. And when we did discover them, it took ages before we clearly understood them and were able use them to our benefit.

The result, or effect, of God's existence is life itself. God is the cause, and life is the result or effect. To believe that life appeared without a creative spiritual cause is the same as believing that a lamp turns on without electricity. God is the unseen life force behind everything, whether we can see it or not.

The Big Bang Theory (the scientific theory, not the television show) points to an ever-expanding universe. The Big Bang was not an actual explosion as many people assume, but rather a vast expansion, or release, of extremely condensed material. If this theory is true, and I have no reason to doubt that it is, then where did this condensed material come from in the first place? Something can't be created from nothing. It all has to start somewhere, from some original source or cause.

The cause or source of all life is out there somewhere. Call it whatever you wish: *Spirit, Universal Mind, The Creator.* But we can easily put our faith in this Higher Power by simply acknowledging life in its multiple forms, and recognizing the ingenious rhythm and harmony of the earth and the cosmos. Life exists because life was created by an unseen conscious force of logic and love.

49

Unity

t's easy to feel isolated from the rest of humanity. We live in a digital age where everyone seems entirely focused on their cell phones and computers. Many of us feel a deep sense of loneliness and estrangement from our communities and each other. We're like a family that has broken apart and barely spends any time together.

But all people share a common source—a Creator.

If God exists, if there is a first cause of all life, then every one of us comes from this same source. If this is true, then all of us are ultimately connected, a singular family held together by a shared parent. Instead of looking at each other as strangers, we can begin to look at what makes us similar, our common bond. Seen in this light, God becomes the spiritual glue holding us together as one unified creation.

When I first got sober, I remember how separated I felt from everyone and everything. I saw myself as a man completely alone and cut off from the rest of the world. It was a terrible feeling. For most of my life,

I was able to drink away any negative emotions—the consequences be damned.

But now, newly clean, I had to actually experience feelings and emotions without running from them. I was living in Los Angeles at the time, a city crowded with people. But I felt lonelier than I ever had in my entire life. I often became extremely depressed, not wanting to get out of bed or leave my apartment for days at a time.

At one point I began speaking with other people about faith and the nature of God. I was curious to know what other people thought and felt about spiritual matters. What I quickly learned is that most people have some form of faith, however faint, in a Higher Power or spiritual force in the universe. In my experience, complete atheism is rare. Even those who claim to be atheists seem hesitant to insist that there is *nothing* more to life than a random interaction of atoms colliding together.

There seems to be a general consensus by most people that there is *something* more to the physical world in which we live. Deep down, in the furthest recesses of the human psyche, we *know* that there is something more than what we see and feel, here and now. We sense a presence, a familiar echo of someone or something, in back of everything.

As I continued to explore faith in God, this realization that we are all ONE, unified by a common *Creator-Source,* slowly began to change how I felt about other people and myself. It dawned on me, slowly at first, that God is everywhere, in everyone. Jesus said: *"The kingdom of God is within you."*

If God is everywhere, including within us, then our lungs are filled by the same breath of life. The source of one is the source of all. The energy and love of God is in everyone and everything. Even those who ignore God and commit acts of hatred and violence have the same wellspring of life within them, though they choose to reject it.

My view of the world began to shift. When I looked at people, especially strangers, I felt something in common with each one of them. We all come from the same place. We all share the same breath of life. God is the unifying element holding us all together.

I rarely feel that horrible sense of loneliness I used to feel. Every time the feeling returns, I can go outside and look around at all the people in the world, recognizing them as members of my own family, brothers and sisters connected by the same parent in back of everything.

50

Final Thoughts

Many people become obsessed with meditating "correctly" and praying "the right way" instead of just easing into it and finding what works best for them. Modern life is filled with plenty of stress. A spiritual life that involves regular prayer and meditation should not cause any stress in your life.

Incorporating prayer and meditation into your daily routine is one of the easiest, safest and most gratifying ways to free up your mind and relax your body. Think of your daily time in prayer and meditation as an oasis in the desert—moments of peace and joy in an otherwise hectic and sometimes difficult existence.

The simplest way to start your routine is to pick a time each day devoted specifically to prayer and meditation. It should be no different than brushing your teeth or bathing each day. I prefer first thing in the morning. Before I begin my day, I sit on my couch, cross my legs, close my eyes and meditate for 10—15 minutes.

Afterwards, I say a short prayer, thanking God for all of my blessings, including my sobriety, my health and my family. I usually finish my prayer by asking how I can be of service to other people that day. I usually do a shorter version of my morning routine at night, either just before going to bed or while I'm lying in bed, reviewing my day. I also pray a few times throughout day.

My routine is not complicated. Actually, it's very simple most days. There are times when I spend more time in meditation, perhaps 20—30 minutes. But generally speaking, 15 minutes in the morning and a few minutes at night is what works best for me.

The point is, don't stress out over your routine. Develop it over time. Find what works for you and what doesn't. Explore and experiment. Try different methods of meditation and prayer (some of which I've discussed already) and seek out new ones as you progress. This should be a lifetime endeavor, not a quick-fix cure like taking a pill. Make it a part of your life, enjoy the journey, and leave out the stress.

It can be very tempting to judge ourselves when we're learning how to pray and meditate. We might think that we're doing it wrong or that we're not getting the results that we're supposed to be getting. Meditation in particular can be a source of frustration for many people when they're starting out. We sit properly, we focus on our breath, but our mind wanders all over the place and we begin to scold ourselves for doing it all wrong.

As I discussed earlier, when I first began to meditate, I would become extremely frustrated by all the noise in my head. I would force myself to sit in one spot, eyes closed, hyper-focused on my breath, waiting for nirvana and enlightenment to overwhelm me. I couldn't understand why, after five entire minutes of meditation, I wasn't reaching full cosmic awareness.

Inevitably I would begin to judge myself, thinking that there must be something wrong with me. I would wonder, *Why aren't I getting it right? What kind of idiot can't learn how to meditate in five minutes?*

Fortunately, I discovered a book called *Zen Mind, Beginners Mind* by Buddhist Monk, Shunryu Suzuki. This book helped me discard my self-condemnation. In it, Suzuki states that, "In the beginner's mind, there are many possibilities, but in the expert's, there are few." In this classic book on Zen meditation, he goes on to further explain that we should always be like beginners in our practice, and should refrain from judging ourselves.

Once we begin our practice, we are doing it correctly simply by the fact that we are trying!

Prayer and meditation are not sporting events. There is no competition, either with ourselves or others. There are no winners and losers. There is only the experience itself. The journey is the thing. Don't expect answers or enlightenment—just be in the moment.

Allow yourself to learn and grow in your practice without harsh judgement or a need to achieve perfection. As the saying goes, perfect is the enemy of the good. There is no such thing as perfection in prayer, meditation or any other part of our lives. There is only learning, growth and persistence. Don't judge yourself; simply persist and grow.

Don't wait until tomorrow, or next week or some mysterious time in the future. Start today! There's no time as good as now. Starting a daily routine of prayer and meditation might be the best thing you ever do for yourself. I know from my own personal experience that the sooner you start, the sooner you'll wonder how you ever managed without it.

You deserve the best that life has to offer, and your best life begins from within. Don't sit around waiting for an external force to come along and save the day for you. The peace and power you seek is within you.

Make the decision today. You don't have to be a recovering addict to reap the benefits of prayer and meditation. Men and women around the world have been discovering the power of prayer and meditation for thousands of years. Now is the time to begin your journey. Don't wait. Start today.

Be patient. Stay calm and don't judge yourself. There is no such thing as perfection, so enjoy the ride.

May you find serenity.

SEVEN

Prayers

Below I have provided several prayers for easy reference.
They can be used any time you need inspiration.

The Serenity Prayer
God, grant me the serenity
To accept the things I cannot change,
Courage to change the things I can,
And the wisdom to know the difference.

The Lord's Prayer
Our Father in heaven, Hallowed is your name.
Your kingdom come, your will be done,
on earth as it is in heaven.
Give us this day our daily bread,
and forgive us our trespasses,
as we forgive those who trespass against us.
and lead us not into temptation,
but deliver us from evil.

Simple Gratitude Prayer

Thank you for this day and for the breath in my lungs.
Thank you for the opportunity to start a new day
And the chance to search for joy and
happiness wherever I find it.

A Prayer for Kindness

God, may I be of service to you and to others.
May I be available to anyone needing kindness.
May I put others before myself.
May I give, rather than take.
May I always bring the light of love into the world.

A Prayer for Love

May I be loving, kind, and giving to everyone I encounter,
And may they find love in their life today and forever.
Amen.

A Prayer for Compassion

Today may I be kind and compassionate to everyone I meet.
May I be of service to others who need my help.
And may I show respect and love
towards all beings on earth. Amen.

The Prayer of St. Francis of Assisi

Lord, make me an instrument of your peace:
Where there is hatred, let me sow love;
Where there is injury, pardon;
Where there is doubt, faith;
Where there is despair, hope;
Where there is darkness, light;
Where there is sadness, joy.
God, grant that I may not so much seek
To be consoled as to console,
To be understood as to understand,
To be loved as to love.
For it is in giving that we receive,

It is in pardoning that we are pardoned,
And it is in dying that we are born to eternal life.
Amen.

A Prayer for Clarity
Lord, bless me with clarity of mind to see what is important.
Help me to stay focused and to remember
the things that bring me happiness and joy.
No matter what comes my way today,
help me to see my role in your plan,
so that I might help others and find my purpose.
Amen.

A Prayer for Right Action
God, help me to make the right decisions today.
Help me to take the right action in
every encounter and situation.
May I think clearly before I proceed
in every moment of the day.
And may my actions bring positive results
for me and for others. Amen.

A Prayer for Good Health
Thank you, God, for my life.
Thank you for this day.
Thank you for my family and friends.
Thank you for the breath in my lungs.
Thank you for my health and well-being.
Thank you for the beauty in nature.
Thank you for the opportunity to serve others.
May I be a blessing to everyone I meet today.
Amen.

A Prayer for Success
God, today may I be successful in everything that I do.
May I be the best that I can be.
May I always be kind to others and to myself.

May I be kind and compassionate toward every living being.
May I work hard and not worry about the results.
May I live life on life's terms and be filled with joy,
knowing that I tried my best every step of the way.
Amen.

A Prayer for Spiritual Wealth
Lord, bless me with peace, serenity and joy today.
May I always recognize my blessings.
May I face each day with gratitude.
May I meet every challenge with hope.
May I always bring love, compassion
and kindness into the world. Amen

A Prayer for Material Wealth
God, bless me with financial prosperity and abundance.
Help me to achieve wealth enough for
a home, security and comfort.
May I succeed and grow in every part of my life.
May I always be generous and giving
with all that I have been given.
May I always be charitable to those in need.
May I always respect and enjoy all my blessings.
Amen.

A Prayer for World Peace by Ernest Holmes
I know there is but One Mind, which is the mind of God,
in which all people live and move and have their being.
I know there is a divine pattern for humanity
and within this pattern there is infinite harmony and peace,
cooperation, unity and mutual helpfulness.
I know that the mind of humankind,
being one with the mind of God,
shall discover the method, the way, and the means
best fitted to permit the flow of Divine Love
between individuals and nations.
Thus harmony, peace, cooperation, unity,